U0612578

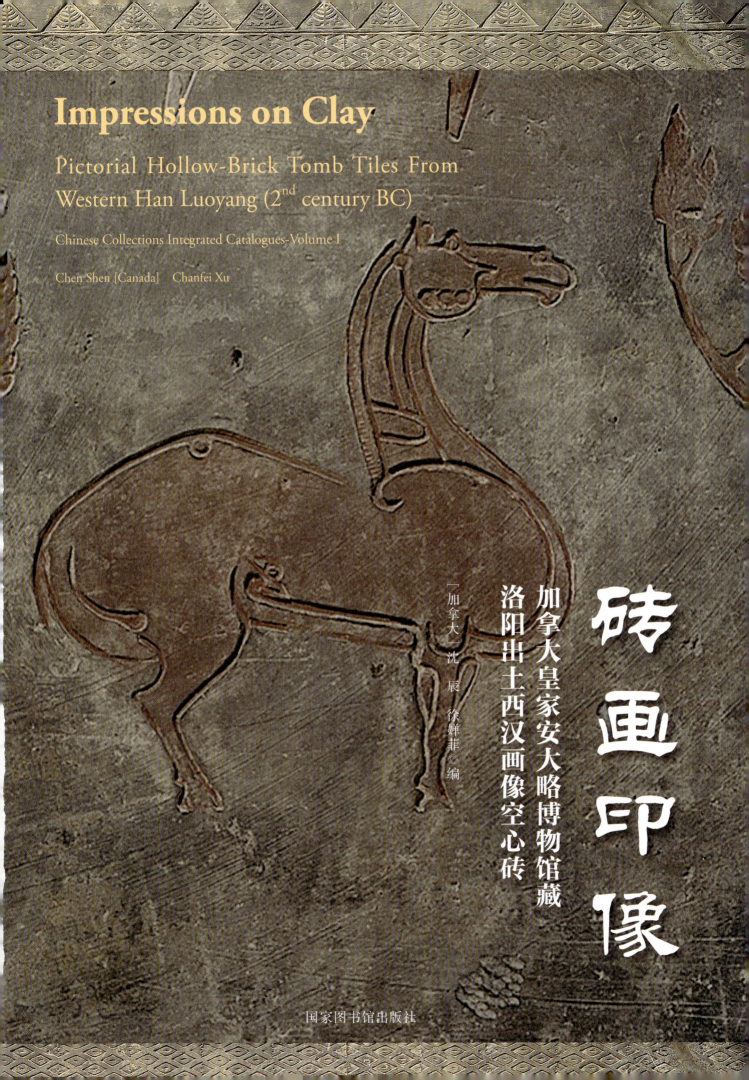

Impressions on Clay

Pictorial Hollow-Brick Tomb Tiles From Western Han Luoyang (2nd century BC)

Chinese Collections Integrated Catalogues-Volume I

Chen Shen [Canada]   Chanfei Xu

砖画印像

[加拿大] 沈 辰 徐婵菲 ◎ 编

加拿大皇家安大略博物馆藏
洛阳出土西汉画像空心砖

国家图书馆出版社

Photos by Lance McMillan and Brian Boyle

本图录得到了 E.Rhodes and Leona B.Carpenter 基金会的慷慨支持

This catalogue is generously supported by the E. Rhodes and Leona B. Carpenter Foundation

砖画印像

Pictorial brick is a type of clay brick with elaborate designs on the surface and used in the construction of underground tomb chambers in ancient China. The surface of the brick presents different portraits of people, animals, and plants through different production methods, such as stamping, carving, and painting, referred to as "pictorial bricks." The bricks found in archaeology are mainly distributed in Henan, Sichuan, Jiangsu, Shaanxi, Shanxi, Shandong and other regions. They have been used from the late Warring States period to the Song and Yuan dynasties. However, the bricks made and used in different periods and regions have different shapes and characteristics.

画像砖是中国古代在建造砖室墓葬中用来装饰墓室的泥制砖块，砖块表面通过不同的制作方式，如印、刻、画等，呈现不同的人物、动物、植物的画像，故称「画像砖」。考古发现的画像砖主要分布于河南、四川、江苏、陕西、山西、山东等地，从战国晚期到宋元时期一直被延续使用，但不同时期和不同地区制作、使用的画像砖均有不同的形制和特点。

目录

第二单元　尚马之风

第三单元　瑞兽祥禽

第四单元　赳赳武夫

附录

Table of Contents

Part Two

Horse-loving Fashion

Part Three

Auspicious Animals and Plants

Part Four

Heroic Warriors

Appendices

概述

沈 辰　徐婵菲

　　画像砖是中国古代在建造砖室墓葬中用来装饰墓室的泥制砖块，砖块表面通过不同的制作方式，如印、刻、画等，呈现不同的人物、动物、植物的画像，故称"画像砖"。考古发现的画像砖主要分布于河南、四川、江苏、陕西、山西、山东等地，从战国晚期到宋元时期一直被延续使用，但不同时期和不同地区制作、使用的画像砖均有不同的形制和特点。比如，汉代的画像砖就有空心大砖和实心小砖两种，前者主要流行于中原地区，后者则多见于四川地区。

　　加拿大皇家安大略博物馆（以下简称 ROM）收藏有 100 多件汉代至宋、金的画像砖，其中汉代的空心大砖数量最多，有 108 块，其余数十件是宋、金时期的实心小砖。藏品中的西汉画像空心砖有出土于洛阳地区的阴纹画像砖和出土于郑州、许昌地区的阳纹画像砖。因为阴纹画像砖仅见于洛阳地区，流传甚少，且制作精美，画像生动，尤显珍贵，在 20 世纪初就深得海外文物藏家和博物馆的垂青，导致一批精致的画像砖流失海外。这里系统介绍的即馆藏的 54 件出土于洛阳地区的阴纹画像空心砖。

一、入藏历史

查阅博物馆典藏记录，ROM 收藏的 108 块汉代画像砖，是在 1914—1931 年间入藏的（参见下表）。

入藏时间（年）	数量（块）	收藏来源
1914	1	罗伯特·蒙德（Robert Mond）爵士捐赠
1918	3	乔治·克劳福斯（George Crofts）
1919	1	乔治·克劳福斯（George Crofts）
1920	4	乔治·克劳福斯（George Crofts）
1922	10	乔治·克劳福斯（George Crofts）
1923	2	乔治·克劳福斯（George Crofts）
1925 年以前	2	乔治·克劳福斯（George Crofts）
1925	3	怀履光（William Charles White）
1926	11	怀履光（William Charles White）
1927	2	怀履光（William Charles White）
1929	11	怀履光（William Charles White）
1931	57	怀履光（William Charles White）
1931	1	日本山中商会捐赠

最早入藏的一块画像空心砖是 1914 年罗伯特·蒙德（Robert Mond）爵士捐赠给博物馆的（图一）。1925 年之前为博物馆征集画像砖的人是英国商人乔治·克劳福斯（George Crofts）。乔治·克劳福斯（1871—1925），爱尔兰裔英国人。1896 年，克劳福斯在中国天津设立永福洋行，经营皮货商贸生意。20 世纪初期中国社会发生剧烈变革，因地缘关系，天津的古玩、艺术品市场异常活跃。克劳福斯利用职业之便从事中国艺术品的收集买卖，成为伦敦古董市场的主要供应商。1918 年，他开始为新成立的 ROM 收集中国文物。1918—1924 年克劳福斯为 ROM 收集了 8000 多件中国文物，其中有汉代画像砖 22 块，包括一对珍贵的上面涂彩的亚腰形空心砖，砖上有浅浮雕的西王母和人物凤鸟画像（图二）。自 1925 年开始，画像砖的收集人是怀履光（William Charles White）。怀履光（1873—1960），加拿大圣公会传教士。1910 年，以中国北方圣公会主教的身份来到河南，定居在开封。

1925 年怀履光接替乔治·克劳福斯，开始为 ROM 收集中国文物。1925—1934 年，怀履光为 ROM 收集了 9000 余件中国文物，其中有汉代画像砖 84 块。1931 年是 ROM 收藏汉代画像砖最多的一年，有 58 块。其中，57 块是怀履光收集的，1 块是日本山中商会捐赠的（图三）[1]。怀履光收集的画像砖中，有 53 块来自洛阳，4 块来自许昌鄢陵。由砖的形制和画像的风格、内容，可以判断山中商会捐赠的画像砖也出自洛阳。所以，1931 年 ROM 共收藏了 54 块洛阳出土的画像砖。

怀履光为什么在一年之内收集到数量如此众多的出自洛阳的阴纹画像空心砖呢？通过整理怀履光与博物馆的往来信件资料，得知这与发生在 1928 至 1932 年的洛阳金村大墓盗掘事件有关，也与怀履光对金村大墓文物的极端喜爱有关。

金村大墓位于河南省洛阳市孟津县平乐镇金村以东，汉魏洛阳故城内城东北部。1928 年夏秋之际的一场暴雨，致使地面塌陷，墓葬暴露，村民自行挖掘，并将所获文物取出售卖。在闻风而来的古董商的鼓动利诱下，当地村民扩大挖掘范围，1929 至 1932 年的三年间，共挖掘 8 座大墓，出土了包括青铜器、玉器、错金银车马器和玻璃器等数千件珍贵文物，其中一套 14 件刻有铭文的骉氏编钟，引起了当时学者的热切关注和讨论。

怀履光听说并得到金村文物是在 1929 年底。1929 年 12 月 16 日，怀履光在写给 ROM 柯雷利馆长的信中说，他从开封古董商蔺士庵那里购得一批包括一件青铜跪坐人像在内的金村文物[2]。在 1930 年 2 月的信件中，怀履光说："又有一件这样青铜跪坐人像文物出现了……这的确是精美无比的艺术品，我一看到它就有志在必得的想法……"在 1930 年 3 月 1 日的信中，怀履光说："我已经关照这位古董商（蔺士庵），要求他为我们保留和这两件青铜人物像一起出土的所有文物，甚至包括残片！"从这三封信件可以看出，怀履光是在 1930 年 2 月收购了两批精美无比的金村文物后，才开始格外留意金村文物，并且对外界表达了要买下所有从金村出土的文物的想法[3]。

1931 年初，蔺士庵为怀履光送来 5 块画像空心砖，称其来自出土骉氏羌钟的金

1　之前我们将这块砖误识为是 1914 年罗伯特·蒙德爵士捐赠，在此予以更正。见［加拿大］怀履光著，徐婵菲译，［加拿大］沈辰校：《中国（洛阳）古墓砖图考》，中州古籍出版社，2014 年。
2　蔺士庵 (1880—1941)，亦称蔺仕庵，字石庵。在开封经营古董商行，是群古斋的店主，基本垄断了当时河南古玩行业的文物生意。
3　［加拿大］沈辰：《金村传说：怀履光和洛阳文物之谜》，《美成在久》2017 年 5 月总第 17 期。

村大墓（也是出土青铜跪坐人像的墓，怀履光将该墓定名为 A 墓）。蔺士庵的话让力求尽收金村出土文物的怀履光非常兴奋，他毫不犹豫地将砖买下。从后来几封写给 ROM 的信中，可以看出怀履光当时的激动心情和对画像砖的喜爱。最早提到画像空心砖是 1931 年 2 月 6 日的信件，信中怀履光告诉博物馆，他刚刚寄出 4 个箱子，其中一些错金银车马器应该是从金村大墓出土的。接着他说，他从蔺士庵那里买下 5 块带画的墓砖，它们有"非常细腻的刻画纹饰，而且特别的是刻有周代或秦代风格的文字，文字应该是表示墓砖在墓中所在位置的。另外，还有用朱笔写上去的古文"。他特别提到，其中一块是持盾武士驭龙画像砖。与 5 块洛阳画像砖同时寄出的还有来自河南许昌鄢陵县汉墓的 4 块空心砖。在接下来的几封信中，怀履光多次提到他在 1931 年底从开封一次性邮出了 36 块画像砖的信息。这说明除上面提到的 5 块画像砖之外，怀履光又收购了 36 块砖。

为博物馆买了这么多画像砖，怀履光自然要向博物馆说明砖的来历和年代。但在当时的情况下，他很难得到准确消息，只能人云亦云。正如他在 1932 年 4 月 4 日的信中所说："从目前的情况看，这批砖有可能来自金村大墓前的祭祀宗庙。此消息来自一位挖墓现场的亲历者。"关于砖的年代，他在 1932 年 4 月 26 日的信中说："明义士先生对骉氏羌钟的铭文做了详细的研究，现在他倾向于将编钟断代到公元前 400 年……要是我们能够确认所有从这个墓出土的遗物都是这个年代，这可能是颠覆性的发现。其实它（指画像砖）本身就是这样了。我们正在小心翼翼地给从这个墓中出来的空心砖装箱，希望马上就可以寄出。"这里提到的正在装箱的空心砖，应该是继第二次的 36 块砖之后又收购的 12 块砖，也就是经怀履光之手收购的 53 块洛阳画像空心砖中余下的部分。

画像砖在从开封寄出之前，怀履光请人都做了拓片，一套寄回多伦多，其余的送给学者研究和鉴赏。在 1932 年 6 月 1 日的信中，他提到："福开森博士和明义士先生都认为它们（画像空心砖）是至今发现的中国早期艺术品中最重要的文物。"他还引用了福开森的话："当我收到你寄来的画像砖拓片时，你不知道我有多高兴。它们太棒了！砖上的龙纹以及驭龙武士的图案是我所见到中国早期艺术中最震撼的东西。这种画像要比武梁祠所见的画像更加精美……他们的确是精彩的发现。"

随着金村大墓的挖掘接近尾声，怀履光对墓葬情况有了一定的"了解"，才知道这些砖与金村大墓并无关系。所以，在 1932 年 9 月 23 日的信中，他告诉博物馆说："这批砖的年代还是个谜。它们应该出土于 A 墓的同一地区，但是不可能出自 A 墓，因为 A 墓中就没有砖。"既然推翻了自己一年多前为博物馆购买画像砖时关于画像砖出处的认识，他总得给博物馆有一个交代，经过他的执着调查，终于打听出画像空心砖的出土地点，这就是他在 1933 年 6 月 29 日写给博物馆的信中所说："现在我知道这批砖是从哪里出来的了。它们是来自 A 墓北部六分之一英里的地处邙山脚下的墓葬中。"此后，怀履光与博物馆的通信中再也没有提到画像砖。

1934 年 3 月，年过花甲的怀履光退休回国。随后，接受加拿大皇家安大略博物馆的聘请担任远东部主任。几年后，又兼任多伦多大学中国研究学系（今东亚系的前身）第一任系主任。在博物馆任职期间，他对自己收集的洛阳画像空心砖资料进行整理研究，1939 年编辑出版了《中国古墓砖图考》。该书的中文版最近已由中州古籍出版社出版 [4]。

二、画砖概览

西汉时期在洛阳地区出现一种新墓型——空心砖墓 [5]，即墓葬是用形制特别的空心砖建成的。空心砖的突出特征有两点：一是体量大，砖的长度 60—190 厘米，宽度（或者高度）20—105 厘米；二是内部空心，因为体量大，为避免入窑焙烧时开裂，故内部空心，所以这种砖称为空心大砖，简称空心砖。空心砖一般有六个面，两个主面（大面）、两个侧面和两个相对较小的端面。根据砖面上有无装饰花纹及花纹的类型，空心砖又被分成素

4　［加拿大］怀履光著，徐婵菲译，［加拿大］沈辰校：《中国（洛阳）古墓砖图考》，中州古籍出版社，2014 年。
5　空心砖墓在战国晚期即已出现，但洛阳发现的最早的空心砖墓是西汉时期的。

面空心砖（无装饰花纹）、几何纹空心砖（只有几何图案）和画像空心砖（有人物、动物、植物等花纹）三类。其中，画像空心砖因流行使用时间短暂、数量少、文化内涵丰富等原因，而备受世人关注。其实，这三类砖的功能一样，都是用于建造墓室的建筑材料。

洛阳画像空心砖为泥质，入窑烧成后呈青灰色，形制规整，质地坚硬而又细腻均匀，砖型主要有长方形和三角形两种。与其他地区画像空心砖相比，洛阳画像空心砖最显著的特征是砖上的画像均为阴纹画像，即构成画像的线条都是低于砖面的阴线。因此，洛阳画像空心砖有时又被称为"阴纹画像空心砖"。但这种阴纹画像不是用尖利的工具刻划出来的，而是用阳纹印模印出来的。因此，这种画像在过去被称为"模印砖画"[6]。

因为考古发掘中至今尚未发现与砖上画像和几何纹饰相同的金属或陶质的印模实物，而有机材料制作的印模又不易保存下来，所以推测印模为木质的。画像通常位于两个主面，整砖画面是由数量不等、大小不一的数种单体画像组合构成的。据统计，ROM收藏的54块阴纹画像砖上，单体画像的种类有人物、马、凤鸟、龙、虎、豹、鹤、雁、猎犬、鹿、兔、猎鹰、朱鹭、鹜、树木、猴等16种，每种单体画像又有多种造型，如人物有15个，马有15个，凤鸟有12个，虎6个，鹤、雁、树木各4个，鹿3个，龙、鹰隼、朱鹭各2个，豹、犬、鹜、兔、猴各1个，各种造型共计有74个（见附录一）。各种单体画像被工匠或精心设计、或随意排布地印在砖上，故而砖上的画面以多种面貌呈现在世人面前，ROM藏空心砖就有42种不同的画面。

依据单体画像之间的关系，砖上的画像可分成两类：一类是单体画像彼此之间没有关联，整体画像给人的感觉是工匠为了填补砖面空白而将画像印上的。比如，印有武士、树木、凤鸟、骏马和虎的砖，印有骏马、凤鸟的砖等，此类画像砖数量最多；另一类是单体画像之间存在着密切关联的砖，如印有手握缰绳的人物画像和马画像的砖，印有挽弓射箭的射手画像和奔鹿画像的砖等，这类砖上的画像显然是工匠按照事先设计好的"图纸"精

6　郭若愚：《模印砖画》，艺苑真赏社，1954年。

心印制的。不论画像之间是否存在关联，作为建墓材料，画像中包含着当时社会流行的丧葬观念与风尚习俗，寄托着生者对逝者的祝福与祈愿，这是毋庸置疑的。

为描述方便，本书将空心砖的两个主面分为 A 面、B 面，大多数空心砖的两面画像是完全一样的，即单体画像的种类和数量相同。少量的空心砖两面画像存在差异，其差异程度不一样。有的砖两面的画像完全不同，如编号 931.13.131 的画像砖，A 面的单体画像是手握缰绳的人物、骏马、树木和凤鸟，主题是驯马；B 面的单体画像是挽弓射箭的人物、双鹿、豹子和猎鹰，主题是狩猎。再如编号 931.13.273 的画像砖，A 面单体画像是彀骑和猛虎，B 面是几何纹图案。有的差异不太明显，两面的单体画像种类相同，仅在数量或排列顺序上稍有不同。

ROM 藏洛阳空心砖，就画像内容而言大体包括三个方面：一是祥瑞辟邪，有龙、凤鸟、虎、豹、连理木、仙鹤以及各种武士等，它们具有趋吉避凶、守护逝者的意义；二是羽化升仙，有龙、武士御龙。另外，凤鸟、仙鹤画像除了具有祥瑞意义外，还与升仙长生有密切关系；三是礼仪风尚，有表现"大蒐礼"和"揖让礼"的田猎、拜谒画像，有表现尚马之风的骏马、天马和驯马画像，有表现尊儒重学风尚的儒生画像，还有表现尚武精神和崇尚建功立业的武士画像与"马上封侯"画像等。其中，田猎画像出现频率比较高，田猎对象有虎、鹿、雁和兔，田猎者有武士、猎犬、猎鹰，甚至还有虎和豹。

田猎表现的是军礼中的"大蒐礼"。"大蒐礼"是西周时期以田猎之名举行的军事演习，同时也是获取各种礼仪活动所需牺牲和礼物的方式之一。《穀梁传·昭公八年》："因蒐狩以习用武事，礼之大者也。"汉代继承了这一传统，但汉代的田猎活动，除了军事意义外，还具有娱乐的性质。如931.13.140 砖上画像表现的是以捕捉鸿雁为目的的田猎活动。鸿雁与人类生活关系非常密切，古人认为雁是一种仁义诚信和志向高远的佳禽，在古代的许多礼仪活动中都用到雁，而且是活雁。《仪礼·士相见礼》中规定："下大夫相见以雁。"《仪礼·士昏礼》中有："纳采纳吉，请期皆用雁。"意思是级别比较低的大夫初次相见时要互相赠送雁，士人结婚从头到尾经过的六道程序（六礼）中有三道程序，男方要给女方送雁。拜谒画像表现的是嘉礼中的贵族相见礼。贵族相见要行揖让礼，"拱手行礼曰揖"。《周礼·秋官》有："司仪掌九仪之宾客、摈相之礼，以诏仪容、辞令、揖让之节。"《汉书·礼乐志》有："揖让而天下治者，礼乐之谓也。" 931.13.137 砖上两位拱手抱拳的人物表现的是"揖让之礼"。这一长一少两位儒生画像，应是西汉汉武帝时期设置的五经博士与博士弟子的形象。

画像空心砖上除了画像，还有几何图案。ROM 藏画像砖上的几何图案也有 7 种 10 余个样式（附录二），它们一般分布在空心砖的主面和侧面上。主面上的几何纹通常位于砖面的边缘，称之为边纹。大多数画像砖只在两条长边的边缘印边纹，边纹的重数一到四重不等，以一重和两重的边纹为多。侧面的几何纹通常位于砖的上侧面（少数砖上下侧面都有），我们称之为侧纹。边纹和侧纹也是用木质印模印制的，它们和画像一样成为画像砖的有机组成部分。

三、画像制作

如前所述，洛阳空心砖上的阴纹画像和边纹、侧纹都是用木质的阳纹印模印出来的，即先有印模，后有画像。因此，制作印模是制作画像的前提和基础。印模和画像是一一对应关系，就是说有多少种单体画像就要制作多少个印模。那么，印模是什么样子？怎样制作的？又是如何使用的呢？

砖上的画像是在砖坯尚处于湿软状态时，由工匠手持印模在确定好的位置像按印章一样印上去的。在用印模按印画像的过程中，工匠一不留神就会出现"差错"。所谓的差错，就是在某些砖上的画像有叠压、重影、深浅不一、线条错位的现象（图四），以及不应出现在砖上的印模边框的痕迹等。然而，也正是因为这些差错，为我们了解印模信息和画像制作情况提供了资料。所以，当我们观看画像砖的时候，在欣赏精彩绝伦的画像之余，还可以饶有趣味地通过观察工匠模印画像时，留在砖上的各种"蛛丝马迹"，去探寻有关画像制作方面的信息。如，工匠在制作一块空心砖上的画像时，使用了多少个印模？哪一个画像先印？哪一个后印？是用同一个印模在砖面上不同的位置一鼓作气地将一种画像全都印出来？还是选择了若干个不同的印模按我们看到的排列顺序穿插着拍印？长达 88 厘米的龙画像是怎么印制的？通过对 ROM 藏空心砖的观察、研究，我们对印模及其使用情况有了更深刻的认识。

1. 印模形制

通过对洛阳考古发现的东周至汉代制陶遗址中出土的陶拍、陶印模资料的整理研究[7]，我们推测制作空心砖画像的木质印模应是用一种材质坚硬、结构细腻耐磨的木材制作的，其形制为：上部是一个便于抓握和按压的捉手，下部是一块有一定厚度的木板，木板的表面雕刻阳纹画像，如图五所示。印模的形状（指下部的木板）多样，总的来说是接近画像的形状。有的印模比较规则，如图六的凤鸟画像印模为长方形，图七的猎犬画像印模似乎也是长方形。有的极不规则，如图八的戟骑画像印模，图九的马画像印模。印模的大小也与画像相差不多，如凤鸟画像印模，凤鸟画像长 9.7 厘米、高 12 厘米，印模长 10.6 厘米、高 15.3 厘米。图七的猎犬画像长 18.2 厘米、高 8.8 厘米，猎犬画像印模，长度不明，高 9 厘米。这种按画像大小、形状设计制作的印模，便于工匠在印制画像时更好地把控画像的间距和高低，有利于工匠制作出画面整齐、好看的画像砖。但形状不规则的印模也有缺点，那就是有可能印出倾斜的画像，比如图十中的马画像。

2. 印模制作

木质印模难以保存，印模上的画像是什么样子，我们已无法看到。但砖上的画像是印模画像的镜像反映，通过砖上的画像可以还原印模上的画像及其制作工序。洛阳空心砖上的画像绝大部分是阴纹画像，即以纯粹的阴纹线条造型的画像，印制这种画像的印模，其制作工序主要有两步：其一，是

7　安亚伟：《东周王城战国至汉代陶窑遗址发掘简报》，《文物》2004 年 7 期；中国社会科学院考古研究所：《洛阳发掘报告》，北京燕山出版社，1989 年。

在平滑的木板上画出画像；其二，是剔除画像之外的部分，只留构成画像的阳纹线条，线条底部的木板是比较光滑的平面。根据砖上画像线条的深度，可知阳纹线条的高度一般 2 毫米左右，最大高度可达 4—5 毫米。此外，洛阳空心砖上还有少量以浅浮雕与阴纹线条相结合的画像，如 931.13.136 砖上的鹤画像，鹤的轮廓线条是阴纹线条，而鹤的身体是浅浮雕，身体上还有表示羽毛的线条（图十一）。这种画像的印模制作起来要复杂一些，除上述两道工序还有第三道，就是将线条底部的木板再向下挖成一个平滑的凹面，在凹面上刻出表示羽毛的线条。用这样的印模印出的画像，会因工匠用力大小不同出现两种艺术效果，用力大是浮雕效果（图十二右边的鹤），用力小是平面效果（图十二左边的鹤）。

大多数画像的印模是用单独一块木板制成的，如树木、猎犬、鹿、鹤和部分人物、马，而尺幅巨大的画像印模则是用几块木板拼接起来的，如龙纹画像。图十三武士御龙画像，龙纹长 88 厘米、高 39 厘米，龙角、龙腹和龙尾三处的线条存在断开和错位的现象，在龙腹、龙尾部位有清晰的印模痕迹（图十四），这些迹象表明这块龙画像印模至少是用四块木板拼接而成，而且四块木板大小、形状都不一样。图十四上卷的龙尾是用两块印模印制的，龙尾前半部后端线条与龙尾后半部前端线条不仅错位而且还有叠压，说明印制龙画像时是按照龙头、龙身再到龙尾的顺序分次印成的。[8]

画像状况反映了印模的制作水平。砖上的画像无不构图准确、神形兼备、个性鲜明、精致美观，生动传神地表现出各种画像的外部特征和内心世界，进而显示印模的制作水平的高超。

3. 印制画像

在备好印模并确定砖上画像和边纹的种类与构图后，工匠开始印制画像。制作步骤为：第一步，工匠用一根细绳印出边纹与画像的分界线。第二步，印制边纹。在分界线之外的边缘区域压印边缘纹饰，有两条或三条边纹的，再印一条绳纹将其分隔。第三步，印画像。模印画像时，先印形体较

8　徐婵菲、［加拿大］沈辰：《见微知著——洛阳西汉阴纹画像空心砖模印技术的痕迹研究》，《故宫博物院院刊》2020 年第 2 期。

大的画像，如树、马和人物等，然后再印较小的画像。个别砖上还有第四步，模印之后，对不满意的画像，工匠还会进行修饰，最典型的一例是编号 931.13.141 田猎砖上的猎犬画像，砖上有四只猎犬，其中一只猎犬的眼部和嘴部经过刮削（图十六），使得眼睛浑圆凸出，嘴部尖利，尤显敏锐、机警。还有编号 931.13.128 砖上的凤鸟画像，也有后期补刻的痕迹。

四、年代推断

粗略统计，自 20 世纪二三十年代至今，阴纹画像空心砖出土数量有数百块[9]，但均为盗掘出土。盗掘者野蛮地挖开古墓，把精致的画像砖带到世人面前的同时，墓葬随之被毁，判断墓葬年代的各种资料信息也丧失殆尽。学者只能依据画像空心砖自身来判断其年代。随着考古资料的丰富，洛阳阴纹画像空心砖为西汉之物已无异议，但其属于西汉一代的哪一时期尚有不同看法，现有的观点有西汉晚期说[10]，西汉武帝至新莽时期说[11]，西汉武帝前后至西汉末年说[12]，西汉早期说[13]，我们依据考古资料、砖上的画像和西汉社会的历史背景等方面的资料，研究认为洛阳阴纹画像空心砖的年代是西汉中期的汉武帝时期。

1. 考古资料

自 20 世纪 50 年代以来，洛阳发掘的西汉墓有数百座，都是规模不大的中小型墓，墓型主要有空心砖墓和土洞墓两种。其中，空心砖墓近百座，时间从西汉早期到王莽时期，但只有一座西汉中期的空心砖墓中出土了阴纹画像空心砖，西汉早期和晚期的墓中均未发现阴纹画像空心砖。

9　两次重要的统计是：1925—1932 年出土数量有二三百块。1977 年，洛阳文物部门收集了 500 多块画像空心砖。分别见郭若愚的《模印砖画》和黄明兰的《洛阳汉画像砖》。
10　周到、吕品、汤文兴：《河南汉画像砖的艺术风格与分期》，《中原文物》1980 年第 3 期，第 8 页。
11　黄明兰：《洛阳汉画像砖》，河南美术出版社，1986 年。
12　吕品：《河南汉代画像砖的出土与研究》，《中原文物》1989 年第 3 期，第 51 页。
13　周到、王景荃：《河南文化大典·文物典·画像砖》，中州古籍出版社，2008 年。

出土画像空心砖的墓位于洛阳市宜阳县牌窑村，1985年发掘。该墓保存完好，由墓道、甬道和墓室组成，甬道和墓室用89块空心砖砌建，墓室为长方形，墓顶为斜坡屋形顶。墓中出土了15块画像空心砖，砖的形制有三角形和长方形两种。随葬器物有铜鼎一件，铜勺一件，铜铺首四件，陶鼎一件，小陶罐二件。由出土文物判定该墓年代是西汉中期稍后[14]。宜阳县牌窑村墓出土的画像空心砖，砖上的画像、几何纹图案的风格、造型，与ROM藏砖的相似度极高，其中的马、树、虎、龙、凤鸟等画像与ROM藏砖相应的画像是用同一个印模印制的，说明两处的砖应是出自同一个作坊，时间相近。

2. 画像资料

最有可能证实年代的画像资料来自砖上数量众多的马画像。ROM藏54块画像砖中有44块墓砖上有马画像，有的砖上甚至只有马一种画像。空心砖上的画像类别，除人物外，造型种类最多的画像也是马画像。马画像的样式有18个，其中独马15个，乘马3个，没有辕马，这说明马是一种有特殊内涵而且非常重要的画像，用马画像装饰砖面是符合当时人们的心理需要的。

画像砖上的龙、凤、虎、鹤等动物画像，因其具有沟通天地、祥瑞辟邪和延年益寿等意义，早在先秦时期就是各种器物上常用的装饰纹样，它们出现在空心砖上比较好理解，但马却不具备上述那些意义，之前很少被用作装饰图案。那么，马为什么会频繁地出现在砖上，而且形式又那么多样呢？

艺术作品往往反映了一个时代所流行、注重的事情，马画像——尤其是艺术夸张类的马画像的出现，一定与西汉中期某一阶段的社会风尚有关系。查阅文献资料可知，这一风尚就是流行于西汉汉武帝时期的尚马之风。

尚马之风的形成，与西汉初期经济凋敝、匈奴时常犯边凌侵的社会状况有关系，更与爱马成癖的汉武帝对良种马的渴望与追求有直接关系。武帝时期对西北地区发动的多次战争，除了要消除匈奴的威胁之外，还有一

14　洛阳地区文管会：《宜阳县牌窑西汉画像砖墓清理简报》，《中原文物》1985年第4期，第5页

个很重要的目的，那就是获取良马以改善汉朝军队的战马素质。受自然条件的限制，中原地区驯养不出优良战马。元朔二年（前127），匈奴入侵，汉遣卫青领兵从云中出击，夺回河套一带，并在那里设置朔方郡。河套地区（今陕西北部、甘肃、宁夏一带的草原地区）自古以来就是适于马匹饲养繁殖的地方，生长于河套地区的马，称河曲马，力气大，耐力强，但是奔跑速度较慢。元狩二年（前121），汉军击败匈奴，获河西地，设立酒泉、武威、张掖、敦煌四郡。河西成为西汉政府重要的养马基地。要改良马匹素质，就需要一定数量的良种马杂交。而身材高大、奔跑迅速的良种马，主要生活在西域乃至中亚地区。

汉武帝很早就知道优良马种要到西北方向寻求[15]。元狩二年（前121）得余吾马和元鼎四年（前113）得渥洼马，数量少，或仅一匹，对改良军马没有意义，武帝只能"朕其御焉"，收归己用。但乌孙马、大宛马却是批量获得（乌孙马千匹，大宛马三千余匹），对改良马种作用巨大。所以，汉武帝自是兴奋不已，见到乌孙马，即称其为"天马"，可见体态之不凡。后来，张骞出使西域归来后，告诉汉武帝大宛国有一种汗血宝马，能日行千里，令汉武帝十分神往，他立即派使者携黄金两千两和一匹金马前往大宛，请求换取。大宛国不仅拒绝换马，还杀了汉使夺了财物。武帝闻知大怒，遂派贰师将军李广利率兵分别于太初元年（前104）和太初四年（前101）两次西征大宛，征讨结果是3000多匹大宛汗血马入长安，见到比乌孙马还要神武健硕的大宛马，汉武帝当即把乌孙天马改名为"西极马"，而将天马的桂冠隆重地赐予大宛马。中亚良马的引入，确实改良了汉朝马匹品种。

得到良马，汉武帝作了两首天马歌，一首是《太一天马歌》，歌曰："太一贡兮天马下，沾赤汗兮沫流赭。骋容与兮跇万里，今安匹兮龙为友。"另一首是《西极天马之歌》，歌曰："天马来兮从西极，经万里兮归有德。承灵威兮降外国，涉流沙兮四夷服。"据王淑梅等考证，《太一天马歌》作于元狩二年，为得余吾马而作；《西极天马之歌》作于元鼎四年，为得乌孙马而

15　"初，天子发书《易》，曰'神马当从西北来'。"《汉书·张骞李广利传第三十一》，中华书局，1962年，第2693页。

作 [16]。从两首《天马歌》中可以看出，汉武帝认为天马是上天赐予大汉帝国的神物，是祥瑞的象征。马在汉代特别是汉武帝时期成为一种具有特殊意义的吉祥动物。

上有所好，下必甚焉。在浓郁的尚马之风影响下，艺术家自然不能也不会做旁观者，他们紧跟时尚，创作出大量有关马的艺术作品。受"事死如事生"观念的影响，尚马之风自然也延伸到地下的墓葬装饰，墓砖上的马画像正是这一风尚的反映。那些造型夸张并画出翅膀的艺术加工型的马，表现的应该就是深受武帝珍爱的来自西北的神马——天马。天马画像，进一步说明了画像空心砖的年代在汉武帝时期，而且距汉武帝获得西域宝马的时间不会太远。

3. 历史背景

画像空心砖出现在汉武帝时期，也有其深刻的社会原因。西汉初期，天下甫定，经济凋敝，民生困苦，恢复经济、发展生产是政府第一要务。在思想文化方面，春秋战国时期的礼仪文化制度尚未恢复，"孝惠、高后时，公卿皆武力功臣。孝文时颇登用，然孝文本好刑名之言。及至孝景，不任儒，窦太后又好黄老术" [17]。丧葬方面，因财力匮乏，加之统治者倡导节俭，举国上下实行薄葬。经过汉初六十余年的恢复发展，至汉武帝即位之时，经济繁荣，国力大增，大一统的政治局面得到巩固。要加强中央集权，实现对地方的有效控制，黄老思想已不能适应统治者的需要，思想上改弦更张的时机业已成熟。汉武帝刚一即位，便开始实施"罢黜百家，独尊儒术"的政策，"建元元年（前140）冬十月，诏丞相、御史、列侯、中二千石、二千石、诸侯相举贤良方正直言极谏之士。丞相绾奏：'所举贤良，或治申、商、韩非、苏秦、张仪之言，乱国政，请皆罢。'奏可" [18]。建元五年（前136）"置五经博士……及窦太后崩，武安君田蚡为丞相，黜黄老、刑名百家之言，延文学儒者以百数，而公孙弘以治《春秋》为丞相，封侯，天下学士靡然乡风矣……为博士

16　王淑梅、于盛庭：《再论汉武帝天马歌的写作缘由和年代问题》，《乐府学》第五辑，第130页。
17　《汉书·儒林传第五十八》，中华书局，1962年，第3592页。
18　《汉书·武帝纪第六》，中华书局，1962年，第155—156页。

官置弟子五十人，复其身。太常择民年十八以上仪状端正者，补博士弟子。郡国县官有好文学，敬长上，肃政教，顺乡里，出入不悖。所闻，令相长丞上属所二千石，二千石谨察可者，常与计偕诣太常，得受业如弟子。一岁皆辄课，能通一艺以上，补文学掌故缺；其高第可以为郎中，太常籍奏。即有秀才异等，辄以名闻……自此以来，公卿大夫士吏彬彬多文学之士矣"[19]。即约从公元前 140 年罢黜百家之言，公元前 134 年官府开始以儒家的经典教义作为培训官员、任用官员的基础和标准，设置博士研习五经（《诗》《书》《礼》《易》《春秋》），并挑选体貌端正的年轻人跟随博士学习，地方上要推选学行兼优之士，赴太常学习，一年后经考核，通一艺以上者，可为候补官吏。自此，为官为吏者多是熟读儒家经书的文质彬彬的士人。

汉武帝推崇儒术的另一举措是"举孝廉"。元光元年（前 134）冬十一月武帝下诏，"初令郡国举孝廉各一人"。师古曰："孝谓善事父母者，廉谓清洁有廉隅者。"[20] 就是按照孝子廉吏的标准向政府举荐人才，被举为孝廉者可以直接进入官吏行列。儒家认为善事父母的标准是："生，事之以礼；死，葬之以礼，祭之以礼。"把养生、送死提到同等的高度。举孝廉之制成为汉代厚葬之风盛行的一只强有力的推手，为博得"孝子"的名声，获得"举孝廉"的机会，一些人不惜财力为逝者举办隆重的丧仪葬礼，建造规模宏大、装饰繁缛的墓葬。洛阳画像空心砖墓即是在这种社会背景下出现的。

五、画像朔源以及艺术风格

画像为什么会在西汉中期出现？它是从何而来的呢？它们又具有什么艺术风格呢？

关于汉代画像的来源，20 世纪 60 年代就有学者指出"战国青铜器上的画像乃是汉画像的真正的先驱"[21]。越来越多的考古资料证实，这一看法是很

19　《汉书·儒林传第五十八》，中华书局，1962 年，第 3593—3596 页。
20　《汉书·武帝纪第六》，中华书局，1962 年，第 160 页。
21　马承源：《漫谈战国青铜器上的画像》，《文物》1961 年 10 期。

有见地的。

用画像反映礼仪制度和社会生活的做法，至迟在春秋战国时期已经发展成熟，现已发现很多春秋战国时期表现人物活动场景的画像，画像的载体有青铜器、漆木器、陶器、绢帛等，其中最典型的当属青铜器（图十七）。据不完全统计，目前发现的装饰有人物活动画像的青铜器有 60 余件，画像内容十分丰富，有宴乐、田猎、射箭、采桑、战争和建筑、树木、鸟兽等。这些画像很大一部分表现的是当时的礼仪活动，如宴乐表现的是燕礼中的饮酒礼、祭礼，射箭表现的是射礼，田猎、战争是军礼等[22]。另一部分表现的是神话故事，如禽鸟走兽。用画像反映社会生活的做法被汉代继承并且发扬光大，在画像内容、载体和表现形式等各方面都有丰富与创新，其中最具代表性的当属画像砖、画像石。

ROM 藏洛阳空心砖上的画像均是用线条表现出来的。以线造型是最古老的绘画方法，也是中国画特有的造型方式。新石器时代的陶器、玉器上就出现了具有一定含义的线刻、线绘符号和花纹，商周时期玉器上圆润流畅的线刻纹饰，让我们看到了匠师掌控、驾驭线条能力的巨大进步。随着时间的推移，人们开始用线条画表现内容更加丰富和复杂的社会生活，如春秋战国时期錾刻在青铜器上具有主题性的人物、动物图画，但此时的图画带有初创期的稚拙之气。洛阳汉砖上的画像为我们展示了线条绘画在西汉时期的发展水平，砖上的画像皆是用简洁、流畅的线条，寥寥数笔，一个个构图准确、神形兼备、个性鲜明的人物、动物形象便呈现出来，显示了当时画师使用线条的技巧是多么娴熟，多么得心应手。汉代画师不仅能用线条表现出画像的形体、结构，还用线条将画像的动态、动势，甚至内心世界的活动也表现出来。

我们通过几个单体画像和几组有关联的画像，来看看汉代匠师高超的艺术水平。图十八揖让图中的两位人物，从两人的头饰可知，左边之人是裹巾的庶人，右边是戴冠、有一定社会地位的贵族。按照礼法，地位低的

22　马承源：《漫谈战国青铜器上的画像》，《文物》1961 年 10 期；贺西林：《东周画像铜器题材内容的演变》，《文博》1989 年第 6 期；扬之水：《诗经名物新证之六——〈小雅·宾之初筵〉》，《中国文化》1997 年第 15、16 期；徐婵菲、姚智远：《周代铜器上錾刻图画综合研究》，洛阳历史文物考古研究所编：《河洛文化论丛》第五辑，国家图书馆出版社，2010 年。

庶人见到贵族，要趋步上前行礼，而尊者面对施礼者也要躬身还礼。工匠在表现这两位人物时，仅用几根弯曲程度不同的线条，就将趋步向前、屈膝折腰、抱拳行礼的平民和微微欠身还礼的尊者形象表现出来，还通过眼睛和嘴部状态进一步表现出两人的心理状态，庶人眉眼带笑、嘴巴张开（似在致辞问候），尊者嘴巴紧闭上扬，这一张一闭将庶人的谦卑之心和贵族的礼让兼怀优越之感生动传神地表现出来。再如造型多样的马画像，无论是写实性的骏马，还是艺术加工型的天马，匠师针对不同的部位运用不同的线条，胸部、臀部用圆滑的曲线以表现马的浑圆体态和丰厚的肌肉，马尾、后腿用硬朗的折线来表现骏马的雄健和有力。

最能体现工匠艺术造诣者，是画像之间存在关联的整幅画面。如图十九田猎图，受砖形限制，工匠在设计制作这幅图画时将画像分成上、下两组。下面一组有两名马弓手和四只鹿，鹿在马弓手的追赶下朝着砖的右下方奔跑。上面一组只有三只鹿，它们侥幸逃过了猎手的追逐，正在向另一个方向奔跑。朝两个方向奔跑的鹿群，使得这幅平面画产生了立体效果，有了纵深感，在解决上部空间局促问题的同时，也把鹿群遭猎手追逐四散奔逃的真实场景表现出来。仔细观察会发现，砖上的七只鹿以同一块印模印出。那么，为什么有的鹿背上有箭，有的却没有呢？这就是工匠的高明之处了。工匠只制作一块背上中箭的鹿纹印模，并用它印制了砖上所有的鹿纹，然后除了弓箭手正前方的那两只鹿纹，其余五只鹿纹在印好后，背上的那支箭被工匠抹掉了（图二十）。工匠在用这块印模印制鹿纹时，不全是端端正正地使用印模，而是根据需要，有意识地扭转了印模方向。这样印出来的鹿，奔跑的方向和俯仰的角度都有了变化，从而消除了重复、单调之感。这幅鹿画像，毫无疑问，是专门为这幅猎鹿图设计制作的。虽然，它也出现在其他砖上，但不过是工匠为了省事借用一下而已。再如图二十一田猎图中的犬和兔，与上面的鹿画像一样，图中所有的犬、兔是用一块印模印制的，之所以没有让人产生重复之感，就是因为工匠在印制画像时，稍微转动了一下印模，使得犬与兔的跑动方向和头的俯仰程度发生了变化，最前面的那只犬咬住了兔子，将田猎活动引向高潮。

　　总之，砖上的所有画像，都是工匠根据需要精心设计制作的。即便是那些出现次数不多，尺寸又特别小的画像，如马驹、朱鹭、兔子、猴子等，工匠也没有因为它们次要、微小而漫不经心，敷衍了事。大多数砖上的画像都是事先规划好的，对于画像的选择、位置、间距和排布，工匠早已了然于心。对于有情节的画面，工匠颇费了一番心思，灵活地运用各种手法——人物、动物的动作、神情，一根绳索，一支弓箭等将单个画像连贯起来，用简单画像将现实生活中的复杂情景表现出来，显示出极高的艺术造诣。

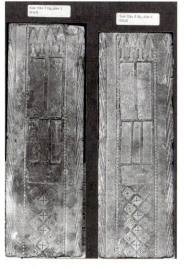 

[图一] 罗伯特·蒙德爵士 1914 年捐赠
给博物馆的画像砖（编号 914.21）

Figure 1. Tomb tile 914.21 was gifted by Sir
Robert Mond in 1914

[图二] 乔治·克劳福斯收集的彩绘画像空心砖
（编号 922.20.625 & 922.20.626）

Figure 2. Two coloured tomb tiles 922.20.625 and
922.20.626 collected by George Crofts

[图三] 日本山中商会捐赠给 ROM 的彩绘画像砖（编号 931.40.1）

Figure 3. Tomb tile 931.40.1 was gifted by the Yamanaka & Co.

[图四] 空心砖上线条错位、深浅不一、重影的画像

Figure 4. Examples of pictorial images that show misaligned lines

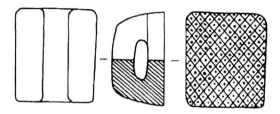

［图五］ 东周王城陶窑遗址出土的陶印模

Figure 5. A woodblock excavated from the kiln of the Eastern Zhou palace

［图六］ 931.13.139 砖上凤鸟画像及印模边框痕迹

Figure 6. The border of the stamp can be observed from this phoenix found on the tomb tile 931.13.139

［图七］ 931.13.135 砖上猎犬画像及印模边框痕迹

Figure 7. The border of the stamp can be observed from this hound found on the tomb tile 931.13.135

［图八］ 931.13.121 砖上骰骑画像及印模边框痕迹

Figure 8. The border of the stamp can be observed from this mounted archer found on the tomb tile 931.13.121

［图九］ 931.13.120 砖上马画像及印模边框痕迹

Figure 9. The border of the stamp can be observed from this horse found on the tomb tile 931.13.120

［图十］ 931.13.264 砖上倾斜的马画像

Figure 10. Skewed pictorial images of the horse can be observed from the tomb tile 931.13.264

［图十一］ 931.13.136 砖上的浅浮雕鹤画像

Figure 11. Example of shallow relief effect depicted on the tomb tile 931.13.136

［图十二］ 931.13.136 砖上的平面鹤画像与浅浮雕鹤画像

Figure 12. Example of shallow relief effect depicted on the tomb tile 931.13.136

［图十三］ 931.13.118 砖上的武士御龙画像

Figure 13. A dragon and a warrior depicted on the tomb tile 931.13.118

［图十四］ 龙腹、龙尾部位清晰的印模边框痕迹

Figure 14. Clear border marks of the woodblock stamp can be observed on the dragon's abdomen and tail

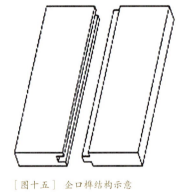

［图十五］ 企口榫结构示意

Figure 15. Example of mortis-and-tenon joint

［图十六］ 931.13.141 砖上经过修饰的猎犬画像

Figure 16. This image of a hound depicted on the tomb tile 931.13.141 shows evidence of manual manipulation

［图十七］ 战国刻纹铜壶（编号 992.169.1）

Figure 17. *Hu* wine vessel dated to the Eastern Zhou dynasty, H 33 x Dia 22 cm, 992.169.1, Dr. Herman Herzog Levy Bequest Fund

[图十八]　931.13.137 砖上的揖让画像

Figure 18. Social etiquette depicted on the tomb tile 931.13.137

[图十九]　931.13.143.B 胡人田猎砖

Figure 19. Scene of mounted archers chasing prey depicted on the tomb tile 931.13.141.B

[图二十]　931.13.143.B 砖上的鹿画像

Figure 20. Images of deer depicted on the tomb tile 931.13.141.B

[图二十一]　931.13.135 砖上的田猎图中的犬和兔

Figure 21. Images of hounds chasing hares depicted on the tomb tile 931.13.135

Introduction

Chen Shen　Chanfei Xu

Pictorial tomb tiles refer to the earthenware bricks with elaborate designs on the surface and used in the construction of underground tomb chambers in ancient China. This form of tomb tiles appeared as early as the Warring State period (5th – 3rd century BC) and continued to be used in the Song dynasty (10th – 13th century). These clay tiles are either stamped, or engraved, or painted, although hardly appeared in a combination of all three methods displaying a rich variety of remarkably artistic images. Depending on the regions or the time periods where and when the tiles were produced, the tomb tiles varied in physical form and decorative motif. In the case of the Western Han dynasty (206 BC – 8 AD), tomb tiles are categorized according to their internal structure, as either solid or hollow. This catalogue focuses on pictorial hollow-brick tomb tiles housed at the Royal Ontario Museum (henceforth ROM), Canada.

The ROM holds more than one hundred pictorial tomb tiles ranging from Han to Song dynasties. The majority of them, a total count of 108, dates to the Han dynasty (206 BC – 220 AD). This catalogue would place our focus on the 54 Western Han pictorial hollow tiles, which were probably unearthed in the city of present-day Luoyang, west of Henan province. Its one-of-a-kind appearance and artistic mastery made these tiles well sought after ever since their discovery at the beginning of the 20th century.

A History of the Collection

All Western Han dynasty tomb tiles at the ROM were acquired between 1914 to 1931 from China. The first one that arrived in Toronto was a gift from Sir Robert Mond in 1914 (Figure 1). From 1918 to 1925, George Crofts (1871 – 1925), an English businessman and an established fur-trader, was responsible for the museum's acquisitions in China. During these seven years, Crofts acquired 22 pictorial tomb tiles, among over 8,000 objects he shipped to Toronto from Tianjin. After 1925, the acquisitions were made by William Charles White (1873 – 1960), when he served as an Anglican Bishop in Henan province. Between 1925 and 1934, Bishop White helped the ROM to collect more than 8,000 Chinese artifacts, which included 84 Han dynasty pictorial tiles.

The year 1931 marked a pinnacle point in the collecting of pictorial tomb tiles, with a total of 58 made in that single year; among which, 54 originated from Luoyang. The correspondences between Bishop White and the museum revealed that such extensive acquisition was driven by clandestine diggings of eight so-called royal tombs in Jincun (a village near Luoyang), during the years of 1928-1932. The Jincun tombs yielded thousands of valuable objects, which had drawn the attention of scholars, museums, dealers, and connoisseurs alike. These objects entered the antique market in early 1929, but it was not until the end of that year when White had heard of them. After two purchases made in early 1930, he grew especially attentive and openly expressed his wish to acquire everything of a Jincun provenance.

In early 1931, a local dealer brought 5 hollow pictorial tomb tiles to White, claiming that they came from Jincun. Convinced of their origin and marvelled by their quality, White took them without hesitation. At the end of the year 1931 and in the following year White had purchased and sent the 53 tomb tiles from Luoyang to the museum. White's affection for these pictorial tiles was shared by his contemporary scholars of Chinese art and culture. Yet White soon learned that these tiles had no association with Jincun, although they did come from tombs in the vicinity – a place called Mangshan, where later archaeologists discovered abundant high-status noble family tombs. In 1939, White published his study of this collection in *Tomb tile Pictures of Ancient China* (White 1939).

Pictorial Tiles at the ROM

During the Western Han period (206 BC – 8 AD), multiple-room tombs constructed with hollow-brick tiles emerged as a popular funerary custom in Luoyang. These tiles are mostly rectangular or triangular in shape; the hollow interior is to reduce weight to accommodate their large size as well as to prevent cracking from the firing. The surfaces of the tile are either left plain, or decorated with geometric patterns and/or pictorial images. The main chamber of these tombs was often decorated with pictorial images on the tiles. The hollow tomb tiles of Luoyang are distinct from those known outside of Luoyang, for all of their surface decorated with intaglio line art – not engraved, but stamped, likely with carved woodblocks.

Images from the Luoyang pictorial tiles housed at the ROM consist of a total of 16 types of motifs, including 77 different kinds of individual variations. Each variation may correspond to one woodblock stamp. Each woodblock thus represents an image of one kind, either an animal (e.g. horse, dragon), a plant (e.g. tree), a person (e.g. warrior), or a geometric pattern. Assuming the same woodblock was used repeatedly, most of the tiles have identical images on the front and the back. However, some do have different degrees of variation. The tile 931.13.273 is an example of different treatments on the two sides: the front depicts a scene of riders and tigers; the back is decorated with geometric patterns. The pictorial images on tomb tiles consisted of either a single modular unit of images or a variety of image units. The units, mirrored by their respective woodblock stamps, can be arranged to form a narrative scene such as hunting or greeting, or just randomly selected as space-fillers. It matters little whether these images tell a story or not, for they carried the auspicious wishes of the living to their beloved deceased. From these images, we can learn much about the burial customs and culture of the Western Han dynasty.

The pictorial decorations identified from the ROM tomb tile collection can be categorized according to their contents. Many motifs are auspicious symbols to ward off evil and protect the dead, such as the dragon, the phoenix, the tiger, the warrior, and the crane. Some tiles have images that are also associated with meanings of longevity and immortality; while other images reflect cultural customs and lifestyle, such as narratives of social etiquette, hunting, and horseback riding. Often, the borders and sides of the tiles are also decorated with geometric patterns, made by the same mechanism of stamping.

Production Method

How were the pictorial tomb tiles made in ancient times? While we know little about them due to loss of production, but we can surely understand that the pictures were impressed with one or more carved woodblock stamps, when the surface of the brick tile was still amendable before drying-out. This method leaves room for human error, as can be seen in Figure 4. Yet, thanks to these marks of imperfection, we can reconstruct how the woodblock stamps were made and used.

The stamps were likely made of hardwood of a dense and smooth texture, with a handle attached to the back of the woodblock (Figure 5). Generally, the shape of the woodblock adheres to the silhouette of the image (Figures 8 and 9); or, they can be rectangular, like those shown in Figures 6 and 7. The image would first be drawn onto the surface of the woodblock, then the negative space would be carved away, creating a depth of about 2 - 5 mm for the lines to leave a deep enough impression on the clay. Occasionally these stamps were given additional modelling to create a shallow relief effect, like the body of the crane on tile 931.13.136 (Figures 11 and 12). Most of the stamps are made of a single woodblock; however, for images of a large size, like the dragon shown in Figure 13, up to four woodblocks are joined by mortise-and-tenon to form a larger stamp (Figures 14 and 15).

After the stamps are prepared and the composition pre-arranged, the stamping process involves three steps. First, a thin rope is used to press a mark of division between the pictorial image and the border. Secondly, the geometric patterns on the borders are stamped. Lastly, the main image is composed: the larger elements would be stamped first, then the smaller elements would follow. Sometimes the craftsmen would manually make corrections and alterations, such as the facial features of one of the hounds on tile 931.13.141 (Figure 16).

Dating the Pictorial Tiles

Since the first quarter of the 20ᵗʰ century, several hundreds of intaglio pictorial hollow tomb tiles have been unearthed. However, because they all came from uncontrolled excavations, all valuable information associated with the context of tombs were no longer available. Thus, the design and the form of the tile itself were probably the only clues museum curators could use to date them before the time when comparative data became available from archaeological sources. Recent archaeological discoveries suggest that most pictorial tomb tiles with similar content and style of pictorial images from the ROM tomb tile collection are from tombs dated to the Western Han. Furthermore, we are able to justify the ROM tiles were produced during the reign of Emperor Wudi, between 140 BC and 87 BC.

In Luoyang, several hundreds of tombs from the Western Han period have been discovered since the 1950s. They are all chambered tombs of medium size, mostly either with an earth-cave structure or constructed with hollow-brick tiles. The dates of the plain hollow-brick tombs ranged from an entire span of the Western Han, but only one single tomb from the middle of the dynasty (likely during the reign of Emperor Wudi) contains pictorial tiles, which were very likely contemporaneous with and made by the same workshop as the pictorial tiles at the ROM.

The horse is one of the most common motifs of the ROM tomb tiles. Both the frequency of their appearance and the variety indicates that the horse was of some significance to the people at the time. Animals such as the dragon, the phoenix, the tiger, and the crane, were widely used as decorative motifs long before the imperial times as they were auspicious symbols. The abundance of the horse motif, which was hardly seen in previous periods, however, was driven only by cultural trends and political concerns during the reign of Emperor Wudi. In the earlier phases of the Western Han, invasions of the Xiongnu nomads from the Eurasian Steppe had long been a major concern to the Han people. Being a sovereign of great military prowess and ambition, Emperor Wudi was particularly fond of horses for they were of great value to warfare. His military campaigns in the northwest frontier were set to acquire high quality breeds to strengthen his military as much as to defend the nation against the threats of Xiongnu. Horse breeding in central China was much constrained by the limits of nature; greater equine breeds from Inner Asia had indeed critically improved the quality of the Han military horses. In fact, when Emperor Wudi first saw the breeds from Inner Asia, he praised them as "heavenly horses" and composed two poems to express his affection and the belief that such horses were a blessing bestowed by the heavenly forces. Image of the winged horse was probably an artistic expression of the "heavenly horse" so praised by the sovereign. Thus, the horse was a very popular symbol of auspicious power during the time of Emperor Wudi.

The emergence of pictorial tomb tiles during this time was also driven by social, economic, and political factors. In early Western Han when the economy was still recovering from the chaos of a transitional period between the old reign to the new, funerary and burial practices were kept humble because the imperial family promoted frugality. During the time of Emperor Wudi, however, Han China experienced an unprecedented time of political stability and economic prosperity. At the same time, his canonization of Confucianism as the philosophical, political, and ritual guideline significantly increased the emphasis on filial piety, which often compelled extravagant burials to express such piety. This ideology and financial availability undoubtedly contributed to the development of tomb tile pictorial representations.

Conclusion: Art of Line

Since the 1960s, scholars have argued that the images of pictorial bronze vessels from the Warring States period were the antecedent of Han pictorial art. In the Eastern Zhou (770 – 256 BC), pictorial images were already fully established media to record and reflect customs and rituals, as well as aspects of society and daily life, such as the bronze *hu* in the ROM's collection (Figure 17). A great number of images depicting figures and events are found on different media, including bronze vessels, lacquerwares, pottery, and textile; among which, pictorial bronzes are the most representative. Their pictorial contents either describe activities of ritual affiliation, such as banquets, archery, warfare; or they depict motifs of myths and legends, such as mythical animals. This visual language was inherited by pictorial art of the Han dynasty, and epitomized by pictorial tomb tiles and stone reliefs.

Tomb tile pictures exemplify the art of line. The line is the most fundamental element of image-making; it is also the representative feature of Chinese painting. Drawings and carvings on pottery and jades from the Neolithic Age and the Bronze Age demonstrate the use of line as a powerful device of artistic expression. As craftsmanship and technology developed, line art was used to depict more complex subjects. The artistic sophistication of the Luoyang tomb tile pictures proves that line art in Western Han had reached an unprecedented height. The images speak of simplicity, liveliness, and vigour; not only do they convey form and structure, but they also capture action and emotion.

Figure 18 depicts a scene of greeting between a commoner and a member of the aristocracy. With only a few masterfully drawn lines, the humbleness of one and the politeness of the other are expressed by the subtlety in gesture and facial expression. For images of a large spatial scale, such as the hunting scene in Figure 19, the picture plane is divided into two parts to overcome being restricted by the fixed size of the tile. A sense of space and depth is created by angling each individual escaping sika deer, enhancing tension and excitement, conjuring an illusion of reality. The creativity of these pictures is also shown in another detail: even though all the deer were made by one stamp, by erasing some of the arrows after stamping, only two deer in front of the hunters appear to have been shot-making the scene look much more vivid and dynamic. Even the smaller and less significant motifs were carefully made. The layout and composition of the image were also carefully arranged. Through the clever use of visual devices such as the movement of the figure, each motif connects with one other to create complex narratives of great artistic value.

Part One
Rites and Confucianism

The rise of the Han dynasty (206 BC – 220 AD) brought social order and stability to a 500-year-long period of conflict and war. In the beginning, Han people longing for peace and prosperity found doctrines of Daoism to be profoundly effective by giving the chaotic society a break and allowing people to follow their hearts and instinct to restore societal prowess and confidence. The first fifty-years of the Han dynasty, prior to the reign of Emperor Wudi (140 – 87 BC), had successfully led Chinese society to enjoy an affluent economy. One of these magnificent changes was reflected in material culture as the emergence of elaborate chamber tombs, which prevailed as a fashionable demonstration of filial piety. Using pictorial tiles to decorate such tombs became a funeral custom among the middle and upper classes.

During the time of Emperor Wudi, Han China experienced an unprecedented time of political stability and economic prosperity. At the same time, Emperor Wudi's canonization of Confucianism as the philosophical, political, and ritual guidelines significantly increased emphasis on filial piety, which often compelled extravagant burials to express such piety. One of the core values advocated by Confucianism was to retain social order by exercising excessive and sophisticated rituals, which was set forth during the Western Zhou period at the beginning of the first millennium BC. Confucianists believed that society must be governed by guidelines of such rites to promote morality and righteousness among its people. Tomb tiles and stone carvings of the Han dynasty frequently feature depictions of Confucian rites that were commonly practiced at the time, as we will see in the following examples, such as the rites of "hunting-and-procession" and "meet-and-greet," among many.

礼仪文化

第一单元

西汉王朝汲取秦代覆亡之教训，政治上广施「仁政」，统治思想「变化因时」，国家很快强盛起来。统治思想在西汉初期先后采用刑名之法、黄老之术，到汉武帝时最终确定为儒家思想。儒术的独尊地位使东周以来崩坏的礼制得以复兴。《汉书·礼乐志》：「乐以治内而为同，礼以修外而为异；同则和亲，异则畏敬。和亲则无怨，畏敬则不争。揖让而天下治者，礼乐之谓也。」就是说，要建设一个和谐统一、有敬畏和亲的社会，必须要有礼制和乐教。

在全盛时期的汉朝，礼制成为治国定邦的基础，礼学是人们进身上层社会的必修知识，礼制精神逐渐深入人心。礼仪文化自然而然就反映在当时的精神生活和各种物质形式上。从今天的考古发现来看，表现各种礼仪内容的画像常见于汉代的墓室壁画、画像石和画像砖上。当然，汉代的礼仪在性质和功能等方面与周代相比已发生了较大的变化。见于洛阳画像砖上的礼仪有表现「大蒐之礼」和「揖让之礼」的田猎、拜谒画像。

胡彀骑射鹿砖

长 85 厘米　高 90 厘米　厚 15 厘米

怀履光收藏，ROM 编号 931.13.143.A

Tomb Tile Depicting Nomadic Rider
Hunting Deer

Length: 85 cm; Height: 90 cm; Thickness: 15 cm

Bishop William C. White Collection, 931.13.143.A

胡彀骑

此砖一面有画像，另一面为素面。砖上有毂骑和雄鹿两种画像。毂骑头戴尖帽，身穿交领左衽短襦，下穿袴，两腿弯曲紧夹马身，双手张弓欲射。乘马头部前伸、四蹄奋起呈疾驰之状，马有辔头、鞍垫，无马镫。鞍垫是通过胸带、肚带和鞧带固定在马背上。六只雄鹿中只有位于毂骑正前方的三只鹿背上有箭，其余鹿上的箭被抹掉了。从人物的服饰上判断此毂骑为胡人。最上面的鹿前腿叠压边纹，可判定先印边纹，后印画像。边纹为斜线纹。上侧面和低端面印有花纹。

A 面

This is one of a pair of triangular tomb tiles that depicts a hunting scene. Three riders dressed in steppe nomadic clothes are on horseback, chasing a flock of fleeing sika deer, drawing their bows to shoot. Three of the deer have already been shot, and each carries an arrow on its back. Composed with only two motif-mold stamps (one is the horse-and-rider and the other is deer with an arrow on the back), this hunting scene was given much dynamic by varying the direction and angle of each deer, and only leaving the arrows on the deer in front of the hunters. The arrows on the other three deer were purposefully erased to indicate their escape.

A thin border of diagonal line pattern encloses the front; the sides have chequered patterns; the backside is left blank.

上侧面和低端面纹饰

雄鹿

胡骰骑射鹿砖

长 85 厘米　高 90 厘米　厚 15 厘米

怀履光收藏，ROM 编号 931.13.143.B

Tomb Tile Depicting Nomadic Rider Hunting Deer

Length: 85 cm; Height: 90 cm; Thickness: 15 cm
Bishop William C. White Collection, 931.13.143.B

A 面

后部重影的胡毂骑

此砖情况与前页之砖基本相同，唯少一位毂骑，多一只雄鹿。下方毂骑画像出现重影现象，一只鹿画像的后部有印模边框痕迹，边框叠压在下方的毂骑画像上。

砖 画 印像：加拿大皇家安大略博物馆藏洛阳出土西汉画像空心砖

Impressions on Clay: Pictorial Hollow-Brick Tomb Tiles From Western Han Luoyang (2nd century BC)

雄鹿后部的印模痕迹

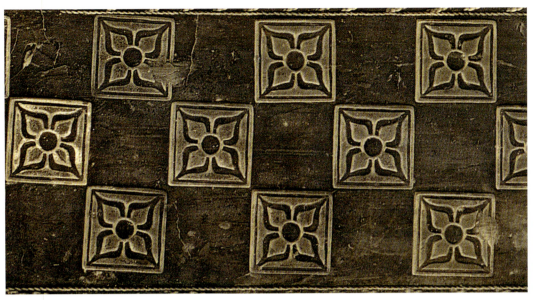

上侧面纹饰局部

This tile pairs with 931.13.143.A. Its similar depiction misses one nomadic rider while adds one more sika deer. The riders' Scythian caps may be the indicator of their ethnicity, or to suggest of a fashion of nomadic lifestyle among the Han people. Marks of the rectangular woodblock stamps can be seen impressed at the lower left corner.

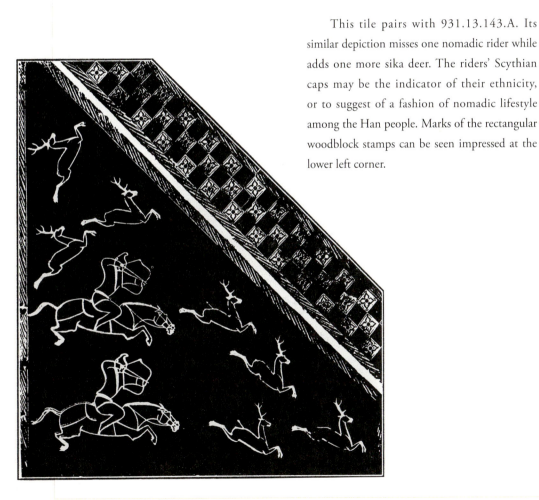

猎犬逐鹿雁砖

长 105 厘米　高 80.5 厘米　厚 17 厘米

怀履光收藏；ROM 编号 931.13.140

Tomb Tile Depicting Hounds
Chasing Prey

Length: 105 cm; Height: 80.5 cm; Thickness: 17 cm

Bishop William C. White Collection, 931.13.140

A 面

两面画像种类相同，但排布有差别。砖面上部是密集的向上斜飞的雁群，下部有两只猎犬和三只雄鹿。因为猎犬的进入，惊飞了雁群、吓跑了雄鹿。此砖表现的是以捕获大雁为主要目的的狩猎活动。猎犬颈带项圈，身形微伏，正悄悄地接近猎物。A面的雁有神色机警，身形微伏，正悄悄地接近猎物。A面的雁有三种型式：一种是只画出一只翅膀的侧面形象的孤雁（I型），它表现的是刚刚飞起的雁；另一种是两只翅膀张开的平面形象的孤雁（II型）；第三种是平面形象的双雁（III型）。B面的雁只有I型、II型两种。A面后面的那只鹿画像后部有印模边框痕迹。上侧面有纹饰。

边纹是勾连云纹。

B 面

下侧面

低端面

Here, the images on both front and back sides are very similar, but not identical. A pair of hounds enter the scene from the lower left, chasing after a mass of fleeing geese and deer. Three variations of the image of the geese make the composition quite vivid and interesting to read. The deer are identical to those stamped on 931.13.143.A and 931.13.143.B, suggesting that they were probably produced from the same workshop.

A border of a slanting-T meander pattern frames the center image.

高端面

I 型雁

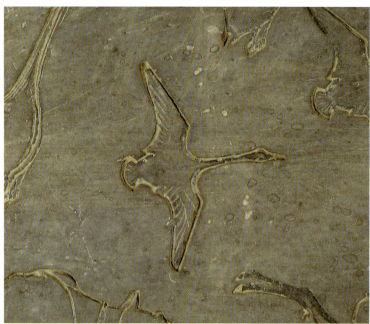

II 型雁

III 型雁

上侧面纹饰

猎犬逐鹿雁砖

Tomb Tile Depicting Hounds Chasing Prey

长 106 厘米　高 80 厘米　厚 17.5 厘米

怀履光收藏，ROM 编号 931.13.141

Length: 106 cm; Height: 80 cm; Thickness: 17.5 cm

Bishop William C. White Collection, 931.13.141

B 面

画像种类与布局与前页砖相同。砖上的一只猎犬印好后，眼睛、嘴部经过刮削处理，其形象更加生动、精彩。

古人认为雁是仁、义、礼、智、信『五常俱全』的佳禽，许多礼仪活动中都要用到雁，而且是活雁，如贵族初次相见时要互相赠雁，士人婚娶时男方要给女方送雁。人们通过田猎活动获取大雁，射礼中的『弋射』，即是为获取活雁而进行的射猎活动。

A面

This tile has a similar composition of stamped images to that of the previous tile 931.13.140. The facial features of one of the hounds were manually enhanced, making it more sculptural.

Bird hunting was a popular sport game during the Eastern Zhou and Han periods. Targets for bird hunting were primarily white goose and widgeon (a freshwater duck). In ancient times, it was customary to present a goose as a meet-and-greet rite as well as a betrothal gift, so goose-hunting using the *yi-she* technique was much in demand. The *yi-she* technique was to shoot the target with an arrow that is attached to an extendable long string, which allows the archer to retrieve the prey by pulling back the string; and certainly, a hound(s) was a part of the game.

猎犬画像

经过修饰的猎犬画像

砖画印像：加拿大皇家安大略博物馆藏洛阳出土西汉画像空心砖

Impressions on Clay: Pictorial Hollow-Brick Tomb Tiles From Western Han Luoyang (2nd century BC)

猎犬逐鹿雁砖

长 105 厘米　高 80.5 厘米　厚 17 厘米

怀履光收藏，ROM 编号 931.13.117

Tomb Tile Depicting Hounds Chasing Prey

Length: 105 cm; Height: 80.5 cm; Thickness: 17 cm

Bishop William C. White Collection, 931.13.117

B 面

画像种类与布局同前页砖相同。

在古代，田猎是一项深受贵族阶层喜爱的活动，并被赋予礼仪的内涵，而且成为训练军队，提高作战技能的一种方式。画像砖上的田猎场面通常表现的是军礼中的『大蒐礼』。『大蒐礼』是西周时期以田猎之名举行的军事演习，同时也是获取各种礼仪活动所需『牺牲』和礼物的方式之一。汉代继承这一传统，但汉代的田猎活动，除了军事意义之外，还具有娱乐的性质。

A 面

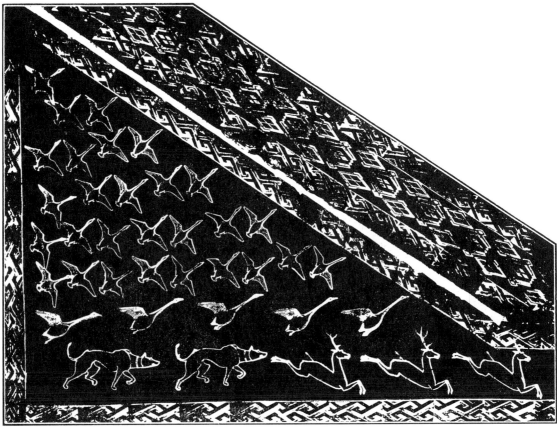

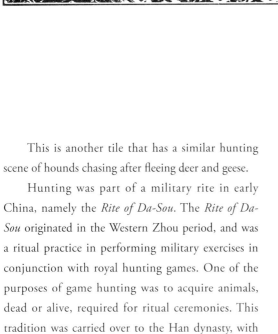

This is another tile that has a similar hunting scene of hounds chasing after fleeing deer and geese.

Hunting was part of a military rite in early China, namely the *Rite of Da-Sou*. The *Rite of Da-Sou* originated in the Western Zhou period, and was a ritual practice in performing military exercises in conjunction with royal hunting games. One of the purposes of game hunting was to acquire animals, dead or alive, required for ritual ceremonies. This tradition was carried over to the Han dynasty, with extra emphasis on competitive entertainment.

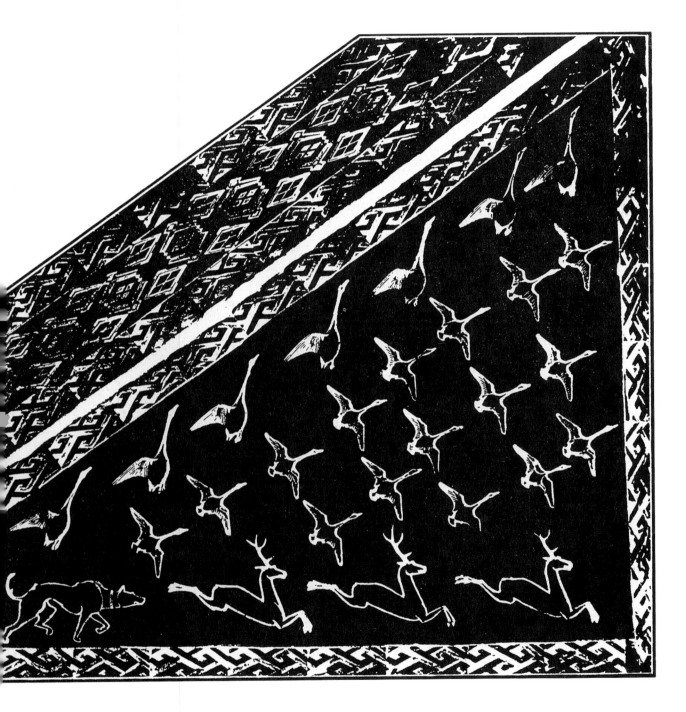

上侧面和低端面

上侧面纹饰

Tomb Tile Depicting Hunting Theme with Leopard/Archer

○ 长 104 厘米　高 85 厘米　厚 17 厘米

◎ 怀履光收藏，ROM 编号 931.13.142.B

Length: 104 cm; Height: 85 cm; Thickness: 17 cm

Bishop William C. White Collection, 931.13.142.B

A 面

两面画像略有差异。一面下部左侧是一只花斑猎豹，它发现了前方的双鹿，正欲追捕；右侧是急速奔跑的雌雄双鹿，外侧的雄鹿昂头奔跑，里侧的雌鹿惊恐地回头张望；上部有一只短尾凤鸟（Ⅰ型）。另一面下部左侧是一位弓箭手，束发，身着袖口和裤管口有纹绣的短襦短裤，腰束带，足穿绚履，呈跪蹲状，上身反转，张弓射箭；上部有两只短尾凤鸟。

边纹是菱格纹。上侧面印有菱格纹。

B面

A 面

双鹿

This triangular tile holds two versions of a hunting theme on its front and back, respectively. On the front, a leopard begins to charge towards a pair of deer, as the stag gallops forward and the doe glances back in fear, with its eyes and mouth wide open. The difference in the size of the predator and the deer creates a convincing illusion of depth of space. In a distance is a phoenix with its beak open, as if making a call of warning. The composition on the other side has a similar layout, but with a pair of fleeing deer, two phoenixes on the top, and an archer of an almost acrobatic pose captured in a moment of anticipation: balanced on one knee and turning back, the archer is just about to loose the arrow.

猎豹

上侧面纹饰

猛虎人物射鹿砖

◎ 长 104 厘米　高 85 厘米　厚 17 厘米

◎ 怀履光收藏，ROM 编号 931.13.142.A

Tomb Tile Depicting Hunting Theme
with Tiger/Archer

Length: 104 cm; Height: 85 cm; Thickness: 17 cm

Bishop William C. White Collection, 931.13.142.A

A 面

此砖情况与前页之砖大致相同。唯 A 面下部
左侧是一只虎（I 型），虎画像的后部有印模边框
痕迹。B 面弓箭手左脚叠压边纹，有重影现象。
边纹是菱格纹。上侧面有菱格纹。

B 面

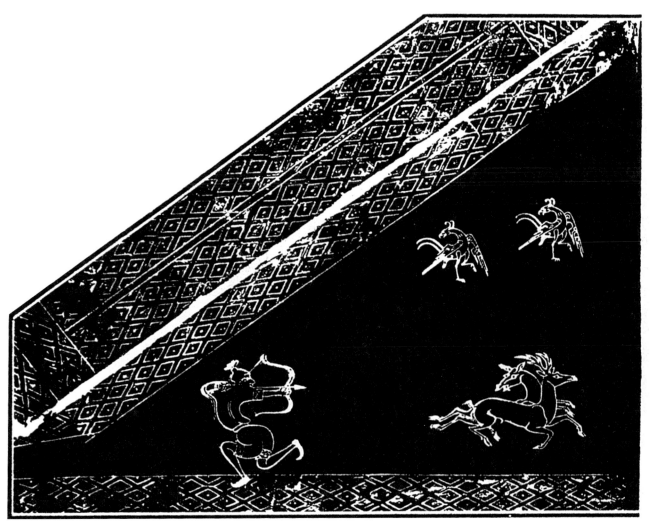

B 面

This tile has an identical composition to that of 931.13.142.B, with stamped images of archer, deer, and phoenix on one side. On the other, the leopard is replaced by a tiger. The border and top are decorated with a pattern of dotted lozenges, similar to the tile shown on the previous page.

A 面

B 面

田猎砖

长 165.5 厘米　高 53 厘米　厚 17 厘米

怀履光收藏，原编号为 931.13.131（B 面）

Tomb Tile Depicting a Hunting Game

Length: 165.5 cm; Height: 53 cm; Thickness: 17 cm

Bishop William C. White Collection, 931.13.131 (Side B)

两面画像完全不同。B面是场面宏大、热闹喧嚣的田猎情景。画面上层是盘旋于空中伺机捕猎的六只猎鹰，猎鹰有两种型式：一种张开双翅（I型）；一种收拢双翅，曲颈勾头俯视下方（II型）。两种猎鹰都是仰视俯视效果，工匠特意表现出猎鹰紧收的腿和蜷曲的爪，以显示其力量。下层左边是弓箭手，其前方有一只猎豹和三对鹿。猎鹰、猎豹已被驯服，它们和猎犬一样是人们田猎活动的绝佳帮手。

A面为驯马画像，见本书第120页。

边纹由勾连云纹和菱格纹组成，宽约8.6厘米。上侧面有纹饰。

Ⅰ型鹰隼

Ⅱ型鹰隼

双鹿

The front and the back of this horizontal tile have completely different images: one is of a groom training his horses, which will be described later (see page 120). Image on the B side, seen here, depicts a grand hunting event. In the sky, six falcons circle above the field, ready to make a dive. On the ground, an archer aims to shoot, while a leopard is charging towards some fleeing deer. In the Han dynasty, animals of prey such as falcons and leopards were tamed and trained to aid in hunting games just like hounds, a common practice for the central court and the vassal states. The images of the archer, deer couple, and the leopard are identical with those on 931.13.142.B, again an indicator of production by the same workshop.

砖画印像：加拿大皇家安大略博物馆藏洛阳出土西汉画像空心砖

Impressions on Clay: Pictorial Hollow-Brick Tomb Tiles From Western Han Luoyang (2ⁿᵈ century BC)

人物射鹿砖

⊙ 长 156 厘米　高 53 厘米　厚 18 厘米

⊙ 怀履光收藏，ROM 编号 931.13.132（A 面）

Tomb Tile Depicting Deer Hunt in a Grove

Length: 156 cm; Height: 53 cm; Thickness: 18 cm

Bishop William C. White Collection, 931.13.132 (Side A)

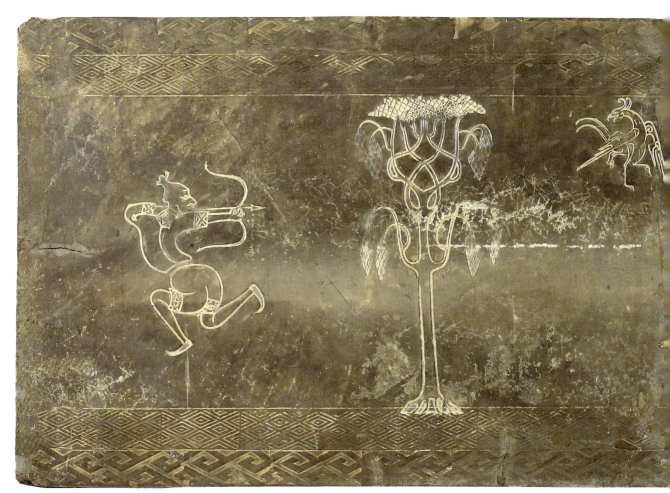

A 面

两面画像完全不同。A面是田猎，画面中有一名弓箭手、一对鹿、一只猛虎（1型）和两棵树（1型），上层有两只短尾凤鸟（1型）。树木根部粗壮，树干笔直，树枝交叉缠绕，并呈对称分布，有的枝头挂着沉重的果实，有的向上伸展到顶部集中形成梯形的平台。有朱书『西北下』三字。B面画像见本书第166页。

边纹由带点菱纹和勾连云纹组成，宽约9厘米。上侧面印有花纹。

上侧面纹饰

洛阳汉画像空心砖

Impressions on Clay: Pictorial Hollow-Brick Tomb Tiles From Western Han Luoyang (2nd century BC)

This is another tile that has two completely different images (see page 166 for Side B). Side A depicts a scene of deer hunt, that same stamps were re-used to produce images of the archer, the deer couple, the tiger, and the phoenix similar to those on tile 931.13.142.A. However, this time the scene is set with a couple of very elaborate and highly stylized trees. The trees are symmetrically designed, with a straight stem, intertwining branches, hanging flowers/fruits, and a dense canopy.

Significantly, there are three hand-written characters in red, " 西北下 " as the phrase that reads "northwest lower." The phrase probably is indicative of the location where the tile was supposed to be placed in the brick tomb chamber.

A 面

砖画印像：加拿大皇家安大略博物馆藏洛阳出土西汉画像空心砖

Impressions or Clay: Pictorial Hollow-Brick Tomb Tiles From Western Han Luoyang (2nd century BC)

毄骑射虎砖

长 121 厘米　高 51 厘米　厚 15 厘米

怀履光收藏，ROM 编号 931.13.121

Tomb Tile Depicting Mounted Archer Hunting Tiger

Length: 121 cm; Height: 51 cm; Thickness: 15 cm
Bishop William C. White Collection, 931.13.121

两面画像一样。有虎（V型）和毂骑两种画像。

毂骑头戴鹖冠，身穿窄袖短襦，腰间束带，下穿大裤，背负羽箭，上身反转，张弓欲射。马做飞奔疾驰之状，马鬃修剪整齐，辔头齐全，马背上的鞍垫用肚带绑缚，鞍垫前后有装饰物，无马镫。虎身上的条纹是S形双钩波磔纹，腹部有三个星纹。A面右边的毂骑前后和上方有印模边框的痕迹。

边纹由菱格纹、嘉禾纹和勾连云纹组成，宽约14厘米。

B面

边纹

On this tile, a captivating moment of a tiger hunt is formulated
through stamping with two woodblocks (a mounted archer and a tiger)
into two pairs of scenes. The mounted archer, adorned in his stylish riding
garment with two tall feathers on the helmet, is turning his head on the
horse to shoot at a roaring tiger coming from the rear. This pictorial scene
is framed by an elaborate border composed of three patterns: a meander, a
triangular crop-like motif, and a dotted lozenge.

砖画印像：加拿大皇家安大略博物馆藏洛阳出土西汉画像空心砖

Impressions on Clay: Pictorial Hollow-Brick Tomb Tiles From Western Han Luoyang (2ⁿᵈ century BC)

A 面

B 面

殼骑射虎朱鹭砖

Tomb Tile Depicting Mounted Archer
with Tiger and Crested Ibis

Length: 128 cm; Height: 52 cm; Thickness: 14.5 cm
Bishop William C. White Collection, 931.13.122

◎ 长 128 厘米　高 52 厘米　厚 14.5 厘米

◎ 怀履光收藏，ROM 编号 931.13.1.22

两面画像种类相同，但排布顺序有差别。有虎（V型）、殼骑和朱鹭三种画像。虎、殼骑画像与前页砖上画像相同。B面殼骑画像上方留有印模边框痕迹。三只朱鹭刻在一块印模上，左右两边的朱鹭面右站立，中间一只单腿站立，扭转脖颈用长喙在整理羽毛。

A面边纹由菱格纹、嘉禾纹和勾连云纹组成，B面边纹中层没有嘉禾纹。

端面

Similar to 931.13.140, this tile has two similar compositions that differ slightly in layout of the impressions made by woodblock stamps. The border and pictorial elements share many similarities with 931.13.121.

A tiger occupies the center of the picture plane, with a mounted archer on the right, and a trio of crested ibis on the left. Standing still, two of the birds gaze forward to the right, another lowers its long beak to clean its coat of feathers, undisturbed by the tense confrontation between man and beast.

B面印模痕迹

A面边纹

砖画印像：加拿大皇家安大略博物馆藏洛阳出土西汉画像空心砖

Impressions on Clay: Pictorial Hollow-Brick Tomb Tiles From Western Han Luoyang (2nd century BC)

A 面

毂骑射虎砖

Tomb Tile Depicting Mounted Archers and Tigers

Height: 112 cm; Width: 50.5 cm; Thickness: 14 cm

Bishop William C. White Collection, 931.13.273

竖砖，高 112 厘米　宽 50.5 厘米　厚 14 厘米

怀履光收藏，ROM 编号 931.13.273

一面有画像，另一面是几何纹。A 面有毂骑和虎（V 型）两种画像，画像上下排布。左、右边纹由菱格纹、嘉禾纹和勾连云纹组成，上部边纹只有一条菱格纹。B 面布满方形的柿蒂纹和十字 S 纹，柿蒂纹边长 3.6 厘米，十字 S 纹长 3.4 厘米、高 3.2 厘米。边纹是斜线纹。

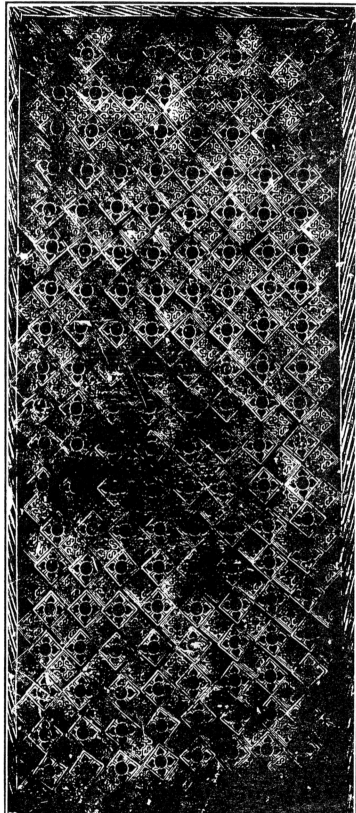

B 面

A 面

B 面

This tile is vertically oriented. On the front, three mounted archers and three tigers are stacked into a single column. Clearly the central scene was simply filled with triple impressions of stamping the two templates that were possibly used on the tile 931.13.121. A chequered pattern formed by two diamond-shaped motifs occupies the back.

A 面

猎犬逐兔天马砖

◎ 长 138 厘米　高 53.5 厘米　厚 17.5 厘米

◎ 怀履光收藏，ROM 编号 931.13.135

Tomb Tile Depicting Horses and Hounds Chasing Hares

Length: 138 cm; Height: 53.5 cm; Thickness: 17.5 cm

Bishop William C. White Collection, 931.13.135

B 面

两面画像和排布略有差别。此砖上部边纹高约29厘米，下部边纹高约4厘米，画像所占面积不到砖面的一半。A面上有猎犬、天马（III型）和狻兔。一群狻兔在群犬的追逐下急速奔逃，最前的一只猎犬咬住了兔子。左边的猎犬和右边的两只兔子留有印模边框的痕迹。B面右边多一只短尾凤鸟（IV型）。

上部边纹由三条纹饰组成，下部边纹是『米』字纹。

上侧面有纹饰。

This tile has very similar compositions on both front and back sides, but one side is much better preserved than the other. The top border is heavily decorated, occupying half of the visual space. The main picture features a dynamic and intense hunt, where one hound on the far right seems to already have locked his jaw onto one of his prey. Other hounds are in pursuit of the bolting hares. Two robust horses divide the hunting scene into three partitions.

A 面

B 面

A 面

猛虎逐鹿砖

Tomb Tile Depicting Tigers Hunting Sika Deer (Fragment)

◎ 残砖，残长 125 厘米　高 51.5 厘米　厚 15.5 厘米

◎ 怀履光收藏，ROM 编号 931.13.119

Remaining length: 125 cm; Height: 51.5 cm;
Thickness: 15.5 cm

Bishop William C. White Collection, 931.13.119

两面画像相同。三条卷草瑞芝纹将砖面分成上下两层，两层的画像相同，都是猛虎（Ⅵ型）逐鹿（Ⅲ型）。猛虎身上的条纹有平行的曲线和 S 形线条，鹿身上有圆形斑点。A 面下层的两只猛虎，一只身形微俯，一只向上跃起，有动画的视觉效果，动感极强。边纹由勾连云纹、双环结纹组成，两条纹饰刻在一块印模上，高约 6 厘米。上侧面有纹饰。

B 面

心砖

上侧面纹饰

Impressions on Clay: Pictorial Hollow-Brick Tomb Tiles From Western Han Luoyang (2nd century BC)

The picture plane is divided into two partitions and framed by three kinds of highly stylized patterns: a meander, a band of interlocking knots, and a repeating design of an abstract, geometric floral motif. The bodies of the escaping sika deer and the prancing tigers are quite fluid and robust, full of energy, a lively moment captured in these simple yet expressive lines.

边纹带有卷草瑞芝纹

野游揖让砖

◎ 长 163 厘米　高 54 厘米　厚 15 厘米

◎ 怀履光收藏，ROM 编号 931.13.137

Tomb Tile Depicting
Social Etiquette

Length: 163 cm; Height: 54 cm; Thickness: 15 cm

Bishop William C. White Collection, 931.13.137

B 面

A 面

两面画像的种类一样，但数量和排列有差别。砖面上层是一行在空中飞翔的大雁，下层是树林（I型），林中有人物、鹤和猎犬在活动。人物有四种形象，均身着深衣，足穿絇履，但头饰、仪态、表情和携带之物不相同。A 面上的人物，左一头戴巾，腰悬长剑，躬身拱手施礼；左二，戴冠，衣袖宽大，颔下生须；左三，戴巾，衣袖宽大，手执一册竹书；右一，戴冠，身体微躬拱手施礼。

根据文献可知，戴冠的是贵族，戴巾的是庶人或未成年人。此砖表现的主题是士族相见揖让之礼仪。西汉时期以右为尊，砖上揖让之礼中，位尊者均在右边。《汉书·礼乐志》有：「揖让而天下治者，礼乐之谓也。」A 面左二、左三的一长一少两位儒生画像，应是汉武帝时期设置的五经博士与博士弟子的形象。

上下边纹是勾连云纹，印模长 10 厘米，宽 4 厘米。上侧面印有纹饰。

A 面

B 面

This tile features two similar pictures that reflect etiquette in social occasions during the Western Han dynasty.

The scene is set in a natural environment: a flock of geese is roaming the sky; several crested ibises are standing among the fruiting trees; a hound is trotting at the edge of the picture plane. Among the flora and fauna are five vividly rendered male figures, shown in profile, each with distinctive features, postures, and accessories.

We see some interactions depicted on the left and the right side, between a repeated figure carrying a long sword and two robed figures wearing caps fastened around the neck. In the Han dynasty, the right-hand side was regarded as superior, thus persons of higher status would be placed on the right. This difference is also shown in the manner of the greeting etiquette: as both parties bow and raise their clasped hands, the person of lower status takes a more pronounced bow. In the case of this image, his facial expression is also much more animated.

This scene reflects a prevalent rite of greet-and-meet amongst Confucian scholars, practiced even when they are out in the field. It is hypothesized that the elder and the youngster here represent a teacher and a student of a school of the study of Confucian Classics, which established during the reign of Emperor Wudi.

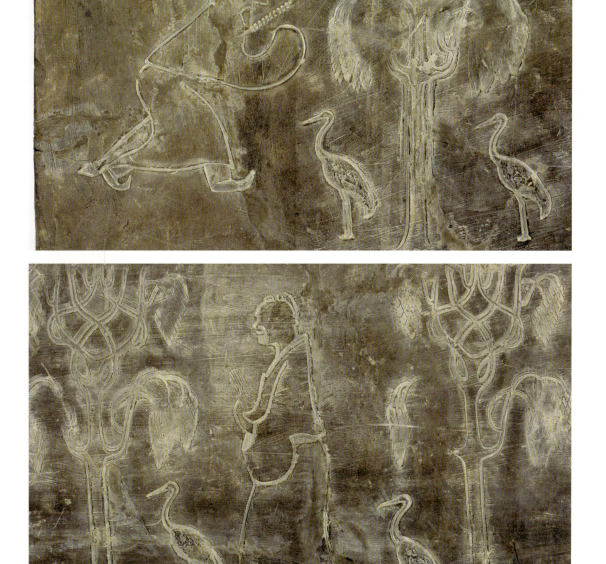

Part Two

Horse-Loving Fashion

The horse is one of the most beloved domesticated animals in ancient China where horseback riding and horse-drawn chariots became a part of the elite lifestyle as early as 3500 years ago. The cavalry was the most powerful military force during the Warring States period (5th – 3rd century BC), which was well represented among the First Emperor underground army of the Qin dynasty (221 – 206 BC). At the beginning of the Han dynasty, horse-breeding became an important domestic endeavor, as the state encouraged peasants to raise horses during times of peace, in preparation for warfare.

Being a sovereign of great military prowess and ambition, Emperor Wudi was particularly fond of horses. One of his intentions to launch his military campaigns and to advocate trades in the northwest frontier was set to acquire high-quality breeds, for enhancing the nation's military prowess as well as for his personal fondness. Emperor Wudi praised the breeds from Central Asia, particularly those from the Ferghana Valley, as "heavenly horses" in his own poems. Under this influence, horse-loving and competition in breeding inevitably became a fashion for the whole nation. Allegedly, if someone was to ride a mare instead of a fine stallion to a gathering, he would be laughed at. This horse-loving fashion during Emperor Wudi's reign led to a flourishing of art images depicting horses, horse-breeding, and horse-related activities, as demonstrated by the following pictorial tomb tiles.

第二单元

尚马之风

在古代，马与人类的关系非常密切。马是农业生产、交通运输的主要动力，也是重要的军用物资，人们对马的喜爱远远超出其它动物，汉代尤其如此。西汉时期为了抵御和消除匈奴侵边的外患，需要建立力量强大的骑兵队伍。建立骑兵的必要条件是要有大量的马匹，所以汉初的几位皇帝都非常重视马政。国家设置专门机构负责马匹的养殖和训练工作。为激励民间养马，汉文帝颁布"复马令"，即百姓家中养一匹马可以免除三人的兵役。一时间帝国上下养马尚马蔚然成风。尚马之风到汉武帝时期尤其炽盛《汉书·食货志》记载"天子（指汉武帝）为伐胡故，盛养马。"当时是"众庶街巷有马，阡陌之间成群，乘牸牝（zìpìn）者摈而不得会聚。"意思是汉武帝为了抗击匈奴大兴养马之风，马匹数量极多，遍布大街小巷、田间地头。当时是家家户户养马，普通百姓出门也有马骑，谁要是骑着母马都不允许参加会聚。为改良马种，汉武帝采取贸易、和亲与战争等多种方式先后从乌孙、大宛等国获取良马。见到威武神俊的西域马种，汉武帝喜不自胜，以"天马"为之命名，并亲作两首《天马歌》，认为天马是上天赐给大汉帝国的神物，是祥瑞的象征。上有所好，下必甚焉，尚马之风遂风靡全国。空心砖上样式多样的马画像，止是当时浓郁的尚马风气的客观反映。

砖画印像：加拿大皇家安大略博物馆藏洛阳出土西汉画像空心砖

Impressions on Clay: Pictorial Hollow-Brick Tomb Tiles From Western Han Luoyang (2nd century BC)

树木吉猴天马砖

长 131 厘米　高 54 厘米　厚 8.5 厘米

日本山中商会捐赠，ROM 编号 931.40.1

Tomb Tile Depicting Geese, Horses, Trees with Monkeys

Length: 131 cm; Height: 54 cm; Thickness: 8.5 cm
Gift of Yamanaka & Co. 931.40.1

116

此砖被锯成两半，只存一面。砖面涂彩。上层是在空中飞翔的大雁（Ⅱ型），下层是树木（Ⅲ型）和天马（Ⅴ型）。天马头部细长，眼睛滚圆，腮部硕大夸张，并有三个圆形斑点，身体浑实饱满，马腿较短。树木右边有一只猴子立在枝杈上。

上边纹由三条纹饰带组成，下边纹是斜线纹。上侧面有纹饰。

Only half of the tile survived, probably caused by the original antiquity dealer who sold this piece twice.

Stamped images of horses, geese, and trees compose a lively yet peaceful scene of nature, perhaps of a horse farm. The branches and leaves of the trees are depicted in a very organic design; their canopies incline slightly towards the side, as if caressed by a light breeze. The horses appear robust and proud, with long, thin necks, their heads held high. Their prominent cheeks are decorated with a row of three circular marks; their bodies are muscular, supported by short legs, making them look rather stout. A monkey squats on top of one of the branches of each tree.

Some areas are painted with sienna and white remain visible, giving us a glimpse of how these tomb tile pictures were decorated.

A 面

驯马砖

长 165.5 厘米　高 53 厘米　厚 17 厘米

怀履光收藏，ROM 编号为 931.13.131（A 面）

Tomb Tile Depicting
Horse Taming

Length: 165.5 cm; Height: 53 cm; Thickness: 17 cm

Bishop William C. White Collection, 931.13.131（Side A）

两面画像完全不同。A面砖面两头各被削去一片，据此可判定此砖是后壁砖，此面朝向墓室。砖面左边是驯马人，中间是两匹相向站立、套着辔头的马（IV型、V型），右边是一只长尾凤鸟（I型）和一棵小树（IV型）。驯马人上部重影，束发插簪，身着交领长襦，领口、袖口有纹绣，腰束带，下着袴，足穿绚屦，手握缰绳。有朱书「上」字，表示此砖位于墓室后壁上层。B面是田猎画面，见本书70页。

边纹由勾连云纹和菱格纹组成，宽约8.6厘米。上侧面有纹饰。

A 面

This is the opposite side of the tomb tile described on page 70, where the image depicts a grand hunt.

This is a tile of the interior wall of the tomb chamber, indicated by two truncated ends. On the left, a horse trainer is holding onto the reins, trying to tame the neighing horse. His mouth opens as if shouting; his body is animated, displaying thorough effort put into this task. Another horse is prancing, as if startled by the action and tension. On the far right, a phoenix stands atop a sapling tree, turning its head back, watching the entire scene.

On the surface, there is a handwritten character in red paint: "上 (upper)."

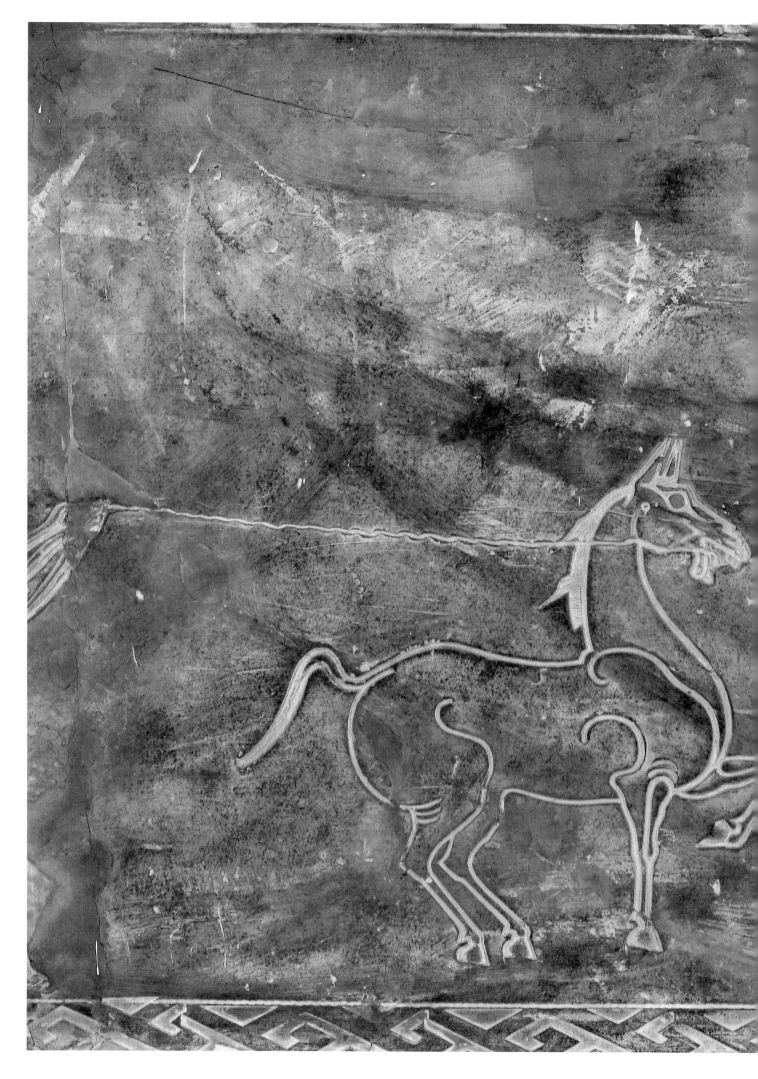

骏马树木虎凤鸟砖

- 长 136 厘米　高 46.5 厘米　厚 14.2 厘米
- 怀履光收藏　ROM 编号为 931.13.266

Tomb Tile Depicting an Equestrian Theme with Tree, Tiger, and Birds

Length: 136 cm; Height: 46.5 cm;
Thickness: 14.2 cm

Bishop William C. White Collection, 931.13.266

A 面

B 面

两面画像种类相同，数量和排布顺序有差别。砖上最引人注目的是树木（I型）、骏马（Ⅷ型、Ⅸ型），树木『顶天立地』，根部粗壮，树冠上部两侧各有一只小鸟，树下有两匹嬉戏的马驹（Ⅷ型、Ⅸ型）。还有三匹成年马（Ⅷ型）、一只虎（I型）和两只长尾凤鸟（Ⅲ型）。A面朱书『西南上』三字；B面有三只凤鸟。此砖画像的表现主题是养马，或许是个养马场。

边纹是菱格纹。

This composition shows a lively scene of a field, possibly a horse farm. A large tree stretches from the ground to the sky, occupying the entire height of the central pictorial space, with two small birds swirling atop. Its lush canopy shades two playful ponies. There are three large, robust horses with stylish manes on the foreground; their muscular bodies, pointed ears, wide-open eyes, and stoic teeth suggest that they were taken great care of. Two phoenixes and a tiger add extra dynamics and mystery to the image.

On this side (or side A) appears three handwritten characters in red paint: " 西南上 " a phrase that reads "southwest upper."

On the opposite side (or side B), the composition is similar with three phoenixes images appear on this side instead of two.

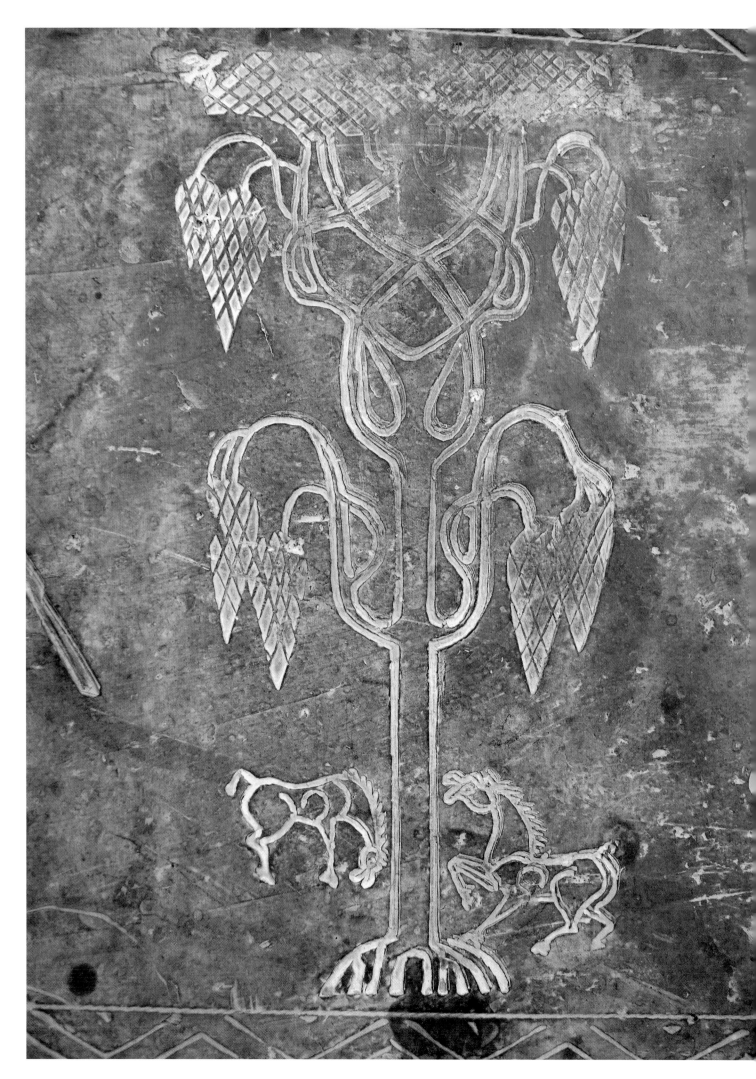

骏马树木虎凤鸟砖

◎ 长 135 厘米　高 46.5 厘米　厚 14 厘米

◎ 怀履光收藏，ROM 编号为 931.13.184

Tomb Tile Depicting an Equestrian Theme with Tree, Tiger, and Birds

Length: 135 cm; Height: 46.5 cm; Thickness: 14 cm

Bishop William C. White Collection, 931.13.184

A 面

画像情况与前页相
同。A面有朱书『东北下』
三字。

砖画印像：加拿大皇家安大略博物馆藏洛阳出土西汉画像空心砖

Impressions on Clay: Pictorial Hollow-Brick Tomb Tiles From Western Han Luoyang (2ⁿᵈ century BC)

B 面

The image is created with the same sets of stamp blocks used to make the tomb tile 931.13.266 (see previous page), with slight differences in composition.

One side has three handwritten red-paint characters : " 东 北下 " a phrase that reads "northeast lower."

A 面

骏马树木虎凤鸟砖

Tomb Tile Depicting an Equestrian
Theme with Tree, Tiger, and Birds

Length: 135 cm; Height: 46 cm; Thickness: 14 cm
Bishop William C. White Collection, 931.13.185

长 135 厘米　高 46 厘米　厚 14 厘米
怀履光收藏，ROM 编号为 931.13.185

画像情况与前页相同。A
面有朱书『东南上』三字。

B 面

The composition is the same as tomb tile 931.13.184 seen on the previous page. All three tiles, 931.13.266, 931.13.184, and 931.13.185, were probably produced from one workshop, indicated by the repeated use of the same stamp blocks.

On one side (or side A) of this tile, there are three handwritten characters in red paint: "东南上" a phrase that reads "southeast upper."

马猎豹鹿砖

◇ 长 142 厘米　高 53 厘米　厚 17 厘米

◎ 怀履光收藏，ROM 编号为 931.13.126

Tomb Tile Depicting a Group
of Animals

Length: 142 cm; Height: 53 cm; Thickness: 17 cm

Bishop William C. White Collection, 931.13.126

A 面

B 面

两面画像不同。A 面上有马（IV 型）、双鹿、猎豹。双鹿、猎豹重影。有朱书『东（南？）』二字；B 面只有马。中间一匹马的尾部留下与马尾形状相近的印模痕迹。

边纹由重边带点菱纹和勾连云纹组成，宽约 9 厘米，重边带点菱纹的印模长 8.8 厘米，宽 4.2 厘米，勾连云纹印模长 10.2 厘米，宽 3.9 厘米。上侧面印有纹饰。

A trio of horses sat on one side of the tile; on the other are animal motifs that we have already seen on other tiles: two horses on each edge, a pair of deer, and a small leopard. Two large characters " 东（南？）" "east, (south?)" are brushed onto the surface, in red cinnabar, in between the horse and the pair of deer on the left.

下侧面孔洞

上侧面

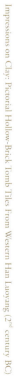

围人天马凤鸟砖

Tomb Tile Depicting Winged Horses with Groom and Phoenixes

长 122 厘米　高 53 厘米　厚 15 厘米

Length: 122 cm; Height: 53 cm; Thickness: 15 cm

怀履光收藏，编号 931.13.139

Bishop William C. White Collection, 931.13.139

两面画像种类相同，数量与排列有差别。画像有天马（Ⅳ型）、围人和长尾凤鸟（Ⅷ型）。天马短脸大眼，腮部硕大，脖子颀长，无鬃，身体饱满壮实，有翼，小尾，马腿与写实性的马相比显得短小，马蹄尤其特别，类兽。围人头戴尖角状的冠，冠前有向上卷翘的突起，冠缨很长，结系后垂緌飘至肩后，身穿长襦大袴，长襦前后襟稍长，足穿絇履，腰悬短剑，左手持上端饰有一旄的长杖，此人应是围人（掌管养马的人）。凤鸟印模痕迹明显。

A面上的围人重影，在其身后有两块压印的图案，身前的两只凤鸟之间也有一块类似的图案。

两面的边纹略有不同，均由三条纹饰组成。从叠压情况可知，先印边纹，后印画像。

A 面

B 面

This tile has an image of an equestrian theme, showing robust, short-tailed winged horses accompanied by grooms and long-tailed phoenix birds. The adornment of the groom figure is depicted with details that are suggestive of an observational nature: a pointed cap with a long tassel hanging over the shoulder; a bell-shaped robe fastened below the waist with a sash; a short sword secured onto the sash; heavy boots; and a long staff topped with an archaic type of small flag made of the tail of cattle.

The wings on the horses' bodies remind us of the story of how Emperor Wudi, greatly pleased by the prowess of horse breeds from Central Asia and their potential aid to the Han cavalry, called them "heavenly horses" and composed two poems.

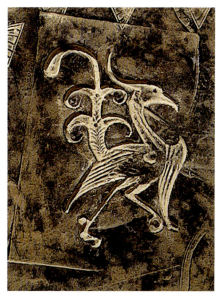

囷人天马凤鸟砖

- 长 115 厘米　高 52.5 厘米　厚 15.8 厘米
- 怀履光收藏，编号 931.13.259

Tomb Tile Depicting Winged Horses with Groom and Phoenixes

Length: 115 cm; Height: 52.5 cm; Thickness: 15.8 cm

Bishop William C. White Collection, 931.13.259

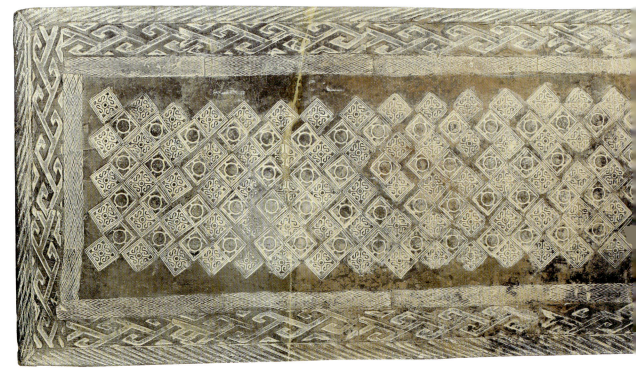

A 面

B 面

一面有画像，另一面是几何纹。A 面画像的种类和型式与前页砖相同；B 面由 4S 方格纹和柿蒂纹组成。4S 方格 3.8 厘米×3.9 厘米，柿蒂纹 3.55 厘米见方。

边纹和前页砖的 B 面边纹相同。边纹由菱格纹、勾连云纹和斜线纹三条纹饰带组成，宽 10.3 厘米。菱格纹印模长 25 厘米，宽 3 厘米。勾连云纹印模长 27 厘米，宽 4.7 厘米。斜线纹，看不出印模的痕迹，最长 8 厘米，短 5 厘米，不平行，一头粗一头细，似为一道一道印制。

One side contains a composition of figures similar to tomb tile 931.13.139; the opposite side is decorated with a chequerboard pattern formed by diamond-shaped motifs. Such side-to-side composition is uncommon. The chequerboard pattern was shaped by repeating individual diamond motifs.

圉人凤鸟砖

◎ 长 115 厘米　高 53 厘米　厚 16 厘米

◎ 怀履光收藏，ROM 编号 931.13.138

Tomb Tile Depicting Groom and Phoenixes

Length: 115 cm; Height: 53 cm; Thickness: 16 cm

Bishop William C. White Collection, 931.13.138

A面

一面有画像，另一面是几何纹。A面有长尾凤鸟（Ⅷ型）和围人两种画像，画像型式和边纹与前页砖上相同。长尾凤鸟印模边框痕迹明显，高15.2厘米。B面几何纹饰与前页砖相同。边纹只有两条几何纹，宽7.5厘米。

On this tile, one side is decorated with the same
patterns as tile 931.13.259 seen on page 150; the
opposite side has an image of alternating motifs: three
grooms and three pairs of vertically stacked phoenixes.

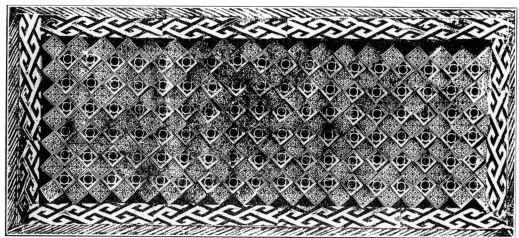

B 面

端面

天马树木吉猴大雁砖

◎ 长 147 厘米　高 53.5 厘米　厚 17 厘米

◎ 怀履光收藏，ROM 编号 931.13.134（B 面）

Tomb Tile Depicting Geese, Horses, and Trees with Monkeys

Length: 147 cm; Height: 53.5 cm; Thickness: 17 cm
Bishop William C. White Collection, 931.13.134 (Side B)

两面画像不同。A面树木武士画像，见248页。B面上层是四对大雁（III型），下层是天马（II型）和树木、猴子。在汉代，猴被认为是能够避除瘟疫、利于马的健康的灵物。

上部边纹由菱格纹、嘉禾纹和勾连云纹组成，宽约12厘米。下部边纹只有菱格纹。上侧面印有纹饰。

Only one side of the tile images is described here, while the pictorial theme on the other side of the tile will be seen in the last section (page 248).

The image is a similar design to that of tomb tile 931.40.1 (page 116), but with some variations in the individual motifs. Here, the geese are arranged in pairs, depicted frontally, as if we are gazing up from the ground to the geese in flight. The horses have prominent cheeks, small ears, and a folded hind leg.

上侧面纹饰

砖画印像：加拿大皇家安大略博物馆藏洛阳出土西汉画像空心砖

Impressions on Clay: Pictorial Hollow-Brick Tomb Tiles From Western Han Luoyang (2ⁿᵈ century BC)

树木人物射虎鹿及骏马砖

◎ 长 156 厘米　高 53 厘米　厚 18 厘米

◎ 怀履光收藏，ROM 编号 931.13.132（B 面）

Tomb Tile Depicting Trees, Horses, Hunting Tiger, and Deer

Length: 156 cm; Height: 53 cm; Thickness: 18 cm
Bishop William C. White Collection, 931.13.132 (Side B)

B 面

两面画像完全不同。A 面是田猎画面，见本书第 74 页。B 面画像模印轻浅，不甚清晰，有骏马（Ⅳ型）、树木和鹤（Ⅰ型）。边纹由重边带点菱纹和勾连云纹组成，宽约 9 厘米。

This is the reverse side of the same tomb tile described on page 74 depicting deer hunt in a grove on the other side.

The image is very lightly stamped. Three horses with a raised front leg are placed among two trees, plus a standing crane with its head up in the air and its beak open, adding an implied auditory element to this simple scene of nature.

Part Three
Auspicious Animals and Plants

Dong Zhongshu (179 – 104 BC) was a renowned Confucian scholar and a minister serving Emperor Wudi. Dong's Confucian doctrinarism, directly advocated and endorsed by the emperor, had a tremendous impact on the culture and lifestyle of Chinese society, which included the reification of auspicious animals and plants. Dong proposed, in praise of the glorious reign of Emperor Wudi, that appearances of certain kinds of animals and plants were an auspicious sign of the righteous reign of an emperor as the son of heaven. Symbols of auspicious animals and plants were usually given abstract names and imaginary forms to make them appear special, such as *jingxing* (jing star), *ganlu* (sweet dew), *zhucao* (vermellion grass), *liquan* (sweet spring water), *jiahe* (fine crop), *fenghuang* (phoenix), *qilin* (unicorn), *qinglong* (green dragon), and *shenma* (heavenly horse), etc.

These auspicious animals and plants were interpreted by Dong and his followers as an ultimate outcome from interactions between heaven and the human-world, or creatures sent by heaven that can transport human souls to the immortal realm. During the Han dynasty, auspicious animals and plants were so exalted that the reign calendar had changed in accordance with the emergences of different auspicious animals and plants. In this section, we will see tomb tile images representing auspicious animals and plants, such as dragons, phoenixes, birds, winged tigers, winged horses, cranes, and longevity trees, etc.

瑞兽祥禽

董仲舒的《春秋繁露·王道》：「王正，则元气和顺、风雨时、景星见、黄龙下……故天为之下甘露、朱草生、醴泉出、风雨时、嘉禾兴、凤凰麒麟游于郊」刘向的《淮南子·览冥训》：「昔者黄帝治天下，……于是日月精明，星辰不失其行，风雨时节，五谷登孰，虎狼不妄噬，鸷鸟不妄博，凤皇翔于庭，麒麟游于郊，青龙进驾，飞黄（神马）伏皂」意思是说如果帝王治国有方，就会风调雨顺，出现景星、甘露、朱草、醴泉、嘉禾、凤凰、麒麟、青龙、神马等祥瑞之物。

为奖有德君王，上天以奇异景，物现于人间作为吉祥征兆的现象，称作祥瑞，也叫符瑞，或符应。祥瑞产生的根源是古代的天人感应思想。西汉时期天人感应思想经儒家学者董仲舒的整理、阐述，祥瑞观念对汉武帝及后世帝王产生了重大影响。祥瑞现象常见于古代文献中。汉武帝在位时即有宝鼎、白麟、芝草、神马、鹿等祥瑞动植物出现。并开了借祥瑞改年号的先河。空心砖上的龙、凤鸟、虎、仙鹤、连理树等画像都是祥瑞之物，具有避除不祥、引魂升仙的作用。

◎ 长 107 厘米 高 81.5 厘米 厚 17.5 厘米

◎ 怀履光收藏，ROM 编号 931.13.186

Tomb Tile Depicting a Dragon and a Warrior

Length: 107 cm; Height: 81.5 cm; Thickness: 17.5 cm

Bishop William C. White Collection, 931.13.186

B 面

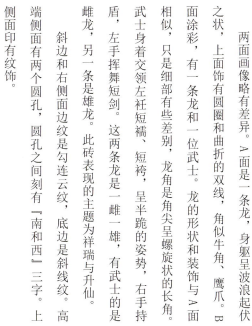

两面画像略有差异。A面是一条龙，身躯呈波浪起伏之状，上面饰有圆圈和曲折的双线，角似牛角、鹰爪。B面涂彩，有一条龙和一位武士。龙的形状和装饰与A面相似，只是细部有些差别，龙角是角尖呈螺旋状的长角。武士身着交领左衽短襦、短袴，呈半跪的姿势，右手持盾，左手挥舞短剑。这两条龙是一雌一雄，有武士的是雌龙，另一条是雄龙。此砖表现的主题为祥瑞与升仙。斜边和右侧面边纹是勾连云纹，底边是斜线纹。高端侧面有两个圆孔，圆孔之间刻有『南和西』三字。上侧面印有纹饰。

A面

上側面纹饰

砖画印像：加拿大皇家安大略博物馆藏洛阳出土西汉画像空

高端面及刻划文字

This design illustrating a dragon carrying its rider, a warrior, is a masterpiece that epitomizes the art of tomb tile pictures in the Western Han dynasty. This simple and efficient composition, of an airborne dragon and a barefoot warrior, is charged with energy and mystery, which may be interpreted as a symbolic representation of the tomb occupant traversing to the realm of afterlife.

The decorative treatment of the dragon hints at the artistic taste of the Zhou dynasty inlaid/gilt design on bronze. Silk paintings in the previous Warring States period used to illustrate a dragon in the form of a boat carrying a Confucian scholar. The tension and movement of the majestic, coiling body of the dragon, and details such as the pronounced snout, tongue, teeth, and the bulging eyes display a life-like quality. The warrior holds in his raised arms a shield and a dagger, charging into afterlife with the protection of the auspicious dragon. This image contrasts the Western concept of the dragon, where in mythology/folklore the heroic warrior is usually depicted fighting and defeating the ferocious, evil beast.

It is also fascinating that the white, red, purple, and blue paints applied to the surface are quite well preserved, both on the intaglio linework and the interior space of the figures, revealing how striking these images once were.

A similar dragon design is depicted on the other side of the tile but missing the warrior.

On the side of the tile, three characters " 南和西 ," incised between the two holds, that read "south and west."

龙纹砖

长 119 厘米　高 62 厘米　厚 16.5 厘米

怀履光收藏，ROM 编号 931.13.118

砖画印像：加拿大皇家安大略博物馆藏洛阳出土西汉画像空心砖

Impressions on Clay: Pictorial Hollow-Brick Tomb Tiles From Western Han Luoyang (2ᵈ century BC)

Tomb Tile Depicting a Dragon

Length: 119 cm; Height: 62 cm; Thickness: 16.5 cm

Bishop William C. White Collection, 931.13.118

B 面

A 面

画像情况与前页之砖相同。龙画像上印
模痕迹明显（详见本书《见微知著》一文）。
由印模痕迹可知，巨大的龙画像至少是用四
块印模组合印制而成。
边纹是菱格纹。上侧面印有菱格纹。

A 面龙首

A 面龙尾部印模痕迹

B 面龙首

The single dragon impression stamped on this tile is identical to that on 931.13.186 on the previous page; disruptions in the linework suggest that this dragon is assembled of at least four stamping blocks (see attached essay in appendix 4).

It appears the dragon image on each side of the tile is slightly different, mainly in the shapes of their horns. Early scholars speculated that this depicts the difference between the gender of the dragon, according to ancient Chinese myths.

砖画印像：加拿大皇家安大略博物馆藏洛阳出土西汉画像空心砖

砖画印像：加拿大皇家安大略博物馆藏洛阳出土西汉画像空心砖

Impressions on Clay: Pictorial Hollow-Brick Tomb Tiles From Western Han Luoyang (2ⁿᵈ century BC)

B 面印模痕迹

182

天马树木鹤雁及猎犬逐鹿兔砖

◎ 长 144 厘米　高 54 厘米　厚 17.5 厘米

◎ "怀履光收藏"，ROM 编号 931.13.136

Tomb Tile Depicting Horses, Trees, Cranes, Geese, and Hound Chasing Prey

Length: 144 cm; Height: 54 cm; Thickness: 17.5 cm

Bishop William C. White Collection, 931.13.136

两面画像种类一样，但排列和数量有差别。A面上层是在空中飞翔的雁群，下层近处是树木（Ⅰ型）、天马（Ⅴ型）、猎犬、鹿和野兔，远处是鹤。大雁和鹤有两种型式。因为印模特别，鹤画像有平面和浅浮雕两种形式，模印浅的是平面效果，深的呈浅浮雕效果。B面的天马（Ⅱ型）与A面的不是同一个印模印制的。

四周边缘是勾连云纹，印模长9.6厘米、宽4.2厘米。上侧面有纹饰。

A 面

B 面

B 面

浅浮雕效果的鹤

A busy scene of nature with three towering trees partitioning the picture plane. In the foreground, two robust horses stand proudly facing the right, their prominent bodies dwarf the hunting scene of a hound preying on a deer and some hares. In the distance stand some cranes, while a row of geese idly flies across the sky.

The backside has a similar composition with a different design of the horse.

上侧面纹饰

边纹

Impression on Clay: Pictorial Hollow-Brick Tomb Tiles From Western Han Luoyang (2nd century BC)

骏马虎凤鸟砖

◎ 长 101.5 厘米　高 45 厘米　厚 14 厘米

◎ 怀履光收藏，ROM 编号为 931.13.127

Tomb Tile Depicting Horses, Tiger, and Phoenixes

Length: 101.5 cm; Height: 45 cm; Thickness: 14 cm

Bishop William C. White Collection, 931.13.127

B 面

A面

两面画像相同。上有骏马（III型）、长尾凤鸟（II型）、虎（IV型）。马头套辔头，马鬃经过修剪，腹部有装饰花纹。虎做回首张望状，身上有双线条纹。A面虎画像在模印时下部用力大，所以虎的四肢线条粗而深，并且留下了印模边框的痕迹。左右两边的凤鸟画像与下方的骏马画像局部有叠压。B面画像模印轻浅，凤鸟画像与上部边纹有叠压。

边纹是菱格纹，印模长10—10.5厘米，宽5.6—6厘米。

砖画印像：加拿大皇家安大略博物馆藏洛阳出土西汉画像空心砖

Impressions on Clay: Pictorial Hollow-Brick Tomb Tiles From Western Han Luoyang (2nd century BC)

Figures of the horse, tiger, and phoenix form a collage in this picture. In the foreground, two horses race across the picture plane, with their heads raised and their manes and tails bouncing; in between, a tiger turns back its head, as if the galloping horses disturbed its pensive stroll. In the background stand a trio of phoenixes, their long tail feathers and wings are designed with minimalistic lines and shapes, yet in an ornate and elaborate manner.

A unique, intriguing pattern adorns the abdomen of the horses; what this pattern signifies is unknown.

砖画印像：加拿大皇家安大略博物馆藏洛阳出土西汉画像空心砖

Impressions on Clay: Pictorial Hollow-Brick Tomb Tiles From Western Han Luoyang (2nd century BC)

A 面

骏马鹤凤鸟砖

◎ 长 118 厘米　高 46 厘米　厚 14 厘米

◎ 怀履光收藏：ROM 编号 931.13.261

Tomb Tile Depicting Horses, Cranes, and Phoenixes

Length: 118 cm; Height: 46 cm; Thickness: 14 cm
Bishop William C. White Collection, 931.13.261

两面画像种类相同。上有鹤（Ⅲ型）、长尾凤鸟（Ⅴ型）、马（Ⅱ型）。画像排布稍显混乱，出现叠压现象，可知先印马画像，再印凤鸟画像，最后印鹤画像。鹤画像是三只鹤刻在一个印模上，大鹤腹中有一条鱼。A面上有『北下』二字，字与画像方向上下相反。

边纹是菱格纹，印模长10.5厘米，宽6厘米。上、下侧面有菱格纹。

A 面

A very busy scene composed of horses, phoenixes, and cranes, each animal in vivid motion. The crane motif is particularly interesting: two large cranes are pacing, their heads forming a niche for their baby fledgling, who is learning how to fly. A fish is depicted in the belly of the parent cranes, a quite fascinating detail that may give us some insights into the Han people's concept of physical space, vision and illusion, and display of visual communication.

One side (or Side A) of the tile has two handwritten characters as "north lower." Interestingly, however, the orientation of the writing is just opposite to that of the figures.

骏马凤鸟砖

◎ 长 114 厘米　高 45.5 厘米　厚 13.5 厘米

◎ 怀履光收藏，ROM 编号为 931.13.120

Tomb Tile Depicting Horses and Phoenixes

Length: 114 cm; Height: 45.5 cm; Thickness: 13.5 cm

Bishop William C. White Collection, 931.13.120

A 面

B 面

两面画像种类与排布相同。上有马（Ⅳ型）、短尾凤鸟（Ⅲ型）。马印模的下边框痕迹明显。边纹是菱格纹，印模长 11.8—12 厘米，宽 6.7 厘米。

The image of this tile is another "terrestrial and avian" theme, with horses and phoenixes. The horses appear to be quite well cared for, with their defined muscle structure, stylishly groomed manes, and upright pointy ears. The phoenixes have short tails and striped body and wings. They appear quite active, perhaps doing a bird song/dance, with their wings flapping, legs spread, heads raised, and beaks open. Gaps disrupting the linework again suggest how individual figures are divided into several stamps.

骏马虎砖

◦ 长 143 厘米　高 54.3 厘米　厚 17.5 厘米

◎ 怀履光收藏　ROM 编印 931.13.264

Tomb Tile Depicting Tigers and Horses

Length: 143 cm; Height: 54.3 cm; Thickness: 17.5 cm

Bishop William C. White Collection, 931.13.264

B 面

A 面

两面画像相同。有虎（II型）、马（IV型）两种画像。因为马画像印模的形状是不规则的，模印画像时方向不易掌握，所以砖上的马画像不同程度存在向下倾斜的现象。

边纹是菱格纹。

On this tile, motifs of tigers and horses are arranged into two rows. Both animals look fierce and tense, with one front leg raised and folded. The horses have pointed, upright ears; big and sharp eyes; open mouths and prominent teeth. The tigers have coats of short stripes; slender bodies; big and round ears; and an evenly striped pattern on the neck that could represent a collar, suggesting that they were tamed and kept as pets or as aid in hunting.

Observation of the stamp impression, such as marks of double stamping and blur on the horses, suggests that the shapes of these stamping blocks were irregular and thus caused uncontrolled force in the stamping process.

虎凤鸟骑吏砖

怀履光收藏：ROM编号为 931.13.128

长 102 厘米　高 47 厘米　厚 14.5 厘米

Tomb Tile Depicting Tiger, Phoenixes, and a Mounted Official

Length: 102 cm; Height: 47 cm; Thickness: 14.5 cm

Bishop William C. White Collection, 931.13.128

A 面

B 面

两面画像相同。上有骑吏、长尾凤鸟（Ⅴ型）和虎（Ⅲ型）。骑吏头戴武弁，上穿宽袖襦，下着大袴，手握缰绳，马呈疾驰之状，马鬃和骑吏的衣袖、袴管向后飘扬，显示马跑之疾速。虎身上有平行的斜线和折角线状的条纹，颈上有项圈，回首张望。长尾凤鸟模印之后，又手工修整。边纹是菱格纹，印模长 10.7 厘米，宽 6 厘米。上侧面有菱格纹。

上侧面

216

The pictorial elements are arranged in two horizontal rows: on the top are three long tailed phoenixes; and on the bottom, a mounted official, a phoenix, and a tiger. The seemingly random composition suggests that this may be one of the tomb tile pictures composed of readily available stamps without any pre-set intension in forming a narrative. From an artistic perspective, the mounted official is particularly intriguing, as his visible leg shows the outline of the belly of the horse, which should have been concealed. This may suggest that these artisans who made this image were not consciously aware of natural laws of the physical world; or, that a mistake was made when carving the stamp, but the artisans chose to ignore it.

天马虎凤鸟砖

◎ 长 134 厘米　高 47 厘米　厚 14.5 厘米

◎ 怀履光收藏，ROM 编号 931.13.263

Tomb Tile Depicting Winged Horses, Tiger, and Phoenixes

Length: 134 cm; Height: 47 cm; Thickness: 14.5 cm

Bishop William C. White Collection, 931.13.263

A 面

B 面

两面画像相同。有短尾凤鸟（Ⅱ型）、天马（Ⅰ型）、虎（Ⅲ型）。边纹是菱格纹，印模长 10.9 厘米，宽 5 厘米。上侧面印两条菱格纹。

砖画印像：加拿大皇家安大略博物馆藏洛阳出土西汉画像空心砖

Impressions on Clay: Pictorial Hollow-Brick Tomb Tiles From Western Han Luoyang (2nd century BC)

左右端面

This is another tile of a simple double-rowed, "land and sky" arrangement composed of images of winged horse, tiger, and phoenix. While all these animals have symbolic meanings such as power and longevity, this kind of composition shows less effort in creating a meaningful scene.

天马虎凤鸟砖

◎ 长 132 厘米　高 46.5 厘米　厚 14.5 厘米

◎ 怀履光收藏，ROM 编号 931.13.182

Tomb Tile Depicting Winged Horses, Tiger, and Phoenixes

Length: 132 cm; Height: 46.5 cm; Thickness: 14.5 cm

Bishop William C. White Collection, 931.13.182

A 面

B 面

两面画像相同。画像种类和型式与前页砖相同。

A面有朱书『东北上』三字。

边纹是菱格纹。上侧面有两条菱格纹。

朱书文字

The picture of this tile is similar in design, with identical individual figures to that of 931.13.263. An increased irregularity in the placement of the phoenix figure, however, makes this composition more dynamic, adding some implication of chaos among the birds.

One side (or Side A) of the tile has three characters " 东 北上 " that reads "east, north, upper" or as a phrase "northeast upper."

砖画印像：加拿大皇家安大略博物馆藏洛阳出土西汉画像空心砖

Impressions on Clay: Pictorial Hollow-Brick Tomb Tiles From Western Han Luoyang (2ⁿᵈ century BC)

天马凤鸟砖

◎ 长 103 厘米　高 46.5 厘米　厚 14 厘米

◎ 怀履光收藏" ROM 编号 931.13.183

Tomb Tile Depicting Winged Horses and Phoenixes

Length: 103 cm; Height: 46.5 cm; Thickness: 14 cm

Bishop William C. White Collection, 931.13.183

A 面

两面画像相同。有短尾凤鸟
（Ⅱ型）、天马（Ⅰ型）两种画像，
型式与前页砖相同。A面上有朱
书「西北下」三字；B面画像模
印轻浅，不甚清楚。
边纹是菱格纹。

B 面

Another "land-and-sky" composition, but with only horses and phoenixes. Parts of the linework of the horses are disrupted, perhaps due to human error or accidents during the production process.

One side (or Side A) of the tile has three characters " 西北下 " that reads "west, north, lower" or as a phrase "northwest lower." It is assumed that this tile might be paired with the one (931.13.182) seen previously and used together for constructing the same burial chamber. The writing here on both tile from craftsmen probably indicated the locations where both tiles should be placed.

天马凤鸟砖

◎ 长 104 厘米　高 47 厘米　厚 14.5 厘米

◎ 怀履光收藏，ROM 编号 931.13.357

Tomb Tile Depicting Winged Horses and Phoenixes

Length: 104 cm; Height: 47 cm; Thickness: 14.5 cm

Bishop William C. White Collection, 931.13.357

A 面

两面画像相同。画像种类
和型式与前页砖相同。

B 面

The picture on this tile has another "land-and-sky" composition of horses and phoenixes, similar to that on the tile of 931.13.183 on previous page 230. The horses show similar disruption in their linework, indicating that these tile pictures were made with the same set of stamps.

Part Four:
Heroic Warriors

Warriors were well respected in ancient China, as they were guardians of the homeland and protectors of family properties. They were heroes of the nation when they were alive, and they were regarded as brave evil spirit fighters in the afterlife. In the year of 123 BC, Emperor Wudi made a special announcement to establish a series of ranks and noble titles awarding warriors who showed their bravery in battle. This special celebration stimulated commoners who sought for higher social status through enlisting their services and demonstrating their heroic acts. Being a warrior became an honourable endeavor in the Western Han.

Hence, the depiction of heroic warriors was common in household decorations, often on the doors or entrances. Book of Han, or *Hanshu*, a classic history of the Han dynasty, recorded a story of Guangchuan Prince Liu Qu placing a portrait of legendary warrior Cheng Qing on the entrance of his palace, as a way of praying for the protection of his family from this warrior. This view in heroic warriors was extended to the Han dynasty funeral practice. Many warrior figures were depicted in the elaborately designed tombs, although not as magnificent as the terracotta warriors accompanying tombs of the First Emperor of Qin and various Emperors of Western Han. Various figures of warriors depicted in the pictorial tomb tiles served similar purposes for middle-upper class members of the society, who wished for an afterlife in peace and prosperity, with the protection from those heroic warriors.

赳赳武夫

《诗经·兔罝》有云："赳赳武夫，公侯干城。"意思是威武雄健的武士，像盾牌和城墙一样，是公侯大人的好护卫。

中国历史上凡是战争频发的时代，崇战尚武的风气就异常强烈。西汉从立国到汉武帝时期，国家一直面临着外有匈奴入侵、内有诸侯叛乱的巨大军事威胁，战事不断。在平定内乱、抗击匈奴的战争中，披坚执锐的将士居功至伟。《汉书·武帝纪》："有司奏请置武功赏官，以宠战士。"即为奖励战争中荣立军功的战士。元朔六年（前123年）汉武帝特设武功爵，按军功大小赏赐爵位，以抬高战士的地位。西汉时期的军功爵制度为庶民阶层获取官爵和利益提供一条便捷之路，故而社会上习武尚武之风十分浓厚。武士在守卫疆土和保护人们安全方面起到了重大作用，受当时社会环境和认知的影响，人们相信武士的画像和龙虎等神兽一样，也具有辟邪、护卫的功能。遂将武士画像也画在宅邸之中。《汉书》记载，广川王刘去的宫殿大门上，画着配备长剑的古代武士成庆的画像。这一做法也延及地下，空心砖尤其是那些可能是墓门设施的砖上装饰有各种样式的武士画像，其用意非常明显，那就是用这些武士画像来保护墓主人免受不祥之物的侵扰。

A 面

持戈武士砖

Tomb Tile Depicting Armed Warriors

Height: 104 cm; Width: 54 cm; Thickness: 14 cm

Bishop William C. White Collection, 931.13.123

竖砖，高 104 厘米　宽 54 厘米　厚 14 厘米

怀履光收藏，ROM 编号 931.13.123

B 面

砖一侧的顶端和底端有方柱形凸起，形同门扉。两面画像相同，有四位持戈佩剑武士（II型）。武士面左，头戴冠，身穿长襦大袴，腰系带，手持长戈，腰间佩剑。冠的样式、冠缨、垂緌清晰。长襦袖子宽大，衣襟前长后短（名曰短后），前襟拽地。足穿前端上卷的鞋。腰带有纹绣。佩剑细长，剑鞘末端镶有剑摽。戈的援与内向上扬起，长胡有穿。戈就是通过胡上的穿用绳索捆绑固定在秘上。

边纹是菱格纹，印模长 10.6 厘米，宽 5.5 厘米。有柱形凸起的一侧侧面印有菱格纹。

This tile is vertically oriented, with two protruding parts on the top and bottom, which may reveal its position and function in the tomb chamber as a gate piece. Framed by two columns of dotted lozenge, the motif of a warrior is repeated four times to form an array. Depicted in profile, he is armed with a tall dagger-axe and a short sword. Likely hung on the belt, the top half of the sword is concealed by the wide sleeve dangling in front. The warrior wears a patterned cap secured under his chin with two short ribbons, and a cross-lapel robe that is longer on the front and shorter on the back, a unique design that might be to offer better protection while allowing movement of the legs. His facial features are rendered with simple lines, but quite descriptive, with a raised brow-ridge, almond-shaped eyes, a round nose, thin moustaches, and thin lips.

侧面纹饰

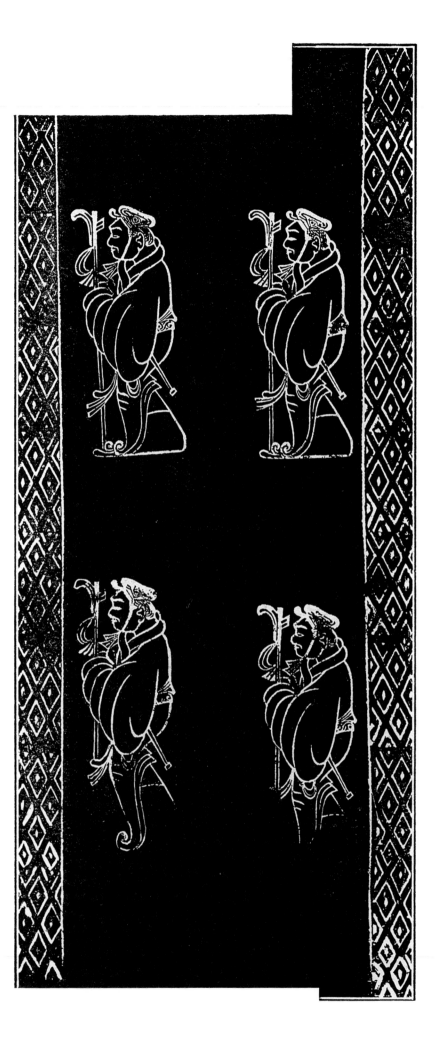

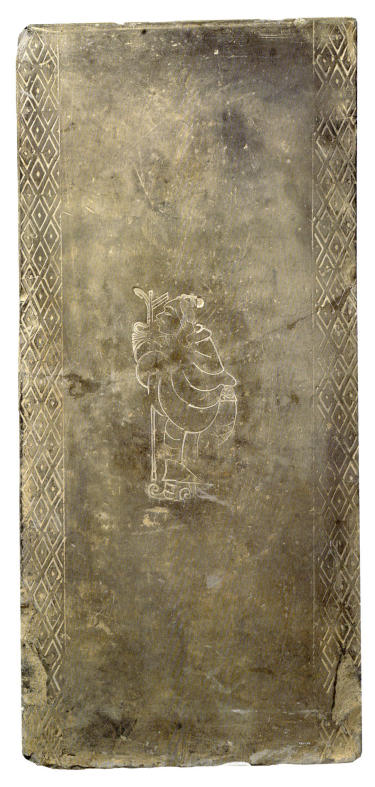

B 面

持戈武士砖

Tomb Tile Depicting a Warrior Holding
Dagger-Axe

Height: 98 cm; Width: 47.5 cm; Thickness: 14.5 cm

Bishop William C. White Collection, 931.13.124

◎ 竖砖，高 98 厘米 宽 47.5 厘米 厚 14.5 厘米

◎ 怀履光收藏，ROM 编号 931.13.124

A 面

两面画像相同。上有一位持戈武士（Ⅰ型），武士面左，头戴冠，颈部有护领，身穿宽袖长襦大袴，腰间束带，腰带上有纹绣，脚穿卷头鞋。手持长戈，戈援与内向上扬起，长胡有穿，通过穿用绳索将戈捆绑在秘上。秘顶端有篿，底端有镦。

左右边纹是菱格纹，印模长11厘米，宽5.7厘米。

This vertical tile is only decorated with two borders of the dotted lozenge and one single figure of a warrior in the center, which is of a similar overall design with the warrior on the tile 931.13.123, but with different details. It is remarkable how attentively rendered this warrior is: the texture of his eyebrow, moustaches, and hair are clearly visible; his calm gaze is vividly depicted; and one of his legs is slightly bent, suggesting motion.

砖画印像：加拿大皇家安大略博物馆藏洛阳出土西汉画像空心砖

Impressions on Clay: Pictorial Hollow-Brick Tomb Tiles From Western Han Luoyang (2ⁿᵈ century BC)

Tomb Tile Depicting Warriors Marching Among Trees and Birds

Length: 147 cm; Height: 53.5 cm; Thickness: 17 cm
Bishop William C. White Collection, 931.13.134 (Side A)

树木吉猴武士砖

◎ 长 147 厘米　高 53.5 厘米　厚 17 厘米
◎ 怀履光收藏，ROM 编号 931.13.134（A面）

A面

两面画像不同。A面上层是四只秃鹫，下层是五位佩剑武士和三棵树木（III型）。武士头戴冠，身穿长襦大袴，足穿绚履，腰间除了腰带另系一根剑带，长剑悬挂于剑带上。为便于活动，长襦的前后襟剪成三角形。树冠右边的枝杈上有一只呈蹲立状的猴子。在汉代，猴是一种吉祥动物，猴与「侯」谐音，逢猴即是「封侯」，预示富贵。B面是天马和树木画像，见本书160页。

上部边纹由菱格纹、嘉禾纹和勾连云纹组成，宽约12厘米。下部边纹只有菱格纹。上侧面印有纹饰（见本书164页）。

This picture is on the reverse side of the same tile described on page 160, which illustrates geese, horses, and trees with monkeys.

On this tile is a scene of five warriors armed with long swords marching among a row of trees, with shrieking birds of prey roaming the sky in the distance. Each tree has a little monkey sitting on a branch in the canopy.

A 面

持戟武士骏马虎凤鸟树木砖

Tomb Tile Depicting Armed Warriors, Horses, Tiger, Phoenix, and Tree

Length: 140 cm; Height: 52 cm; Thickness: 16.5 cm
Bishop William C. White Collection, 931.13.133

长 140 厘米　高 52 厘米　厚 16.5 厘米

"怀履光收藏"，ROM 编号 931.13.133

两面画像种类相同。A面上有持戟武士（Ⅰ型）、虎（Ⅰ型）、树木（Ⅳ型）、短尾凤鸟（Ⅰ型）和马（Ⅳ、Ⅵ型）。持戟武士，面右，戴冠，身穿长襦大袴，足穿绚履，腰间除了腰带，另系一根剑带。双手持戟，腰间佩剑。剑首为圆形，剑柄上的棱脊、剑缑，剑鞘上的剑璏、剑摽清晰，剑带穿过剑璏的细节都刻画得十分真切。树木上方有印模边框痕迹。B面多一位持戟佩剑武士。

边纹是菱格纹，印模长11.1厘米，宽7.4厘米。

B面

砖画印像：加拿大皇家安大略博物馆藏洛阳出土西汉画像空心砖

Impressions on Clay: Pictorial Hollow-Brick Tomb Tiles From Western Han Luoyang (2ⁿᵈ century BC)

A scene of warriors armed with halberds and short swords, two variations of horses, a collared tiger, and a phoenix standing atop a sapling tree. The warrior is depicted in rich details: his facial features are clearly and vividly rendered, showing a sense of character and personality. The garment captures the warrior's body shape and movement, while his weapons are clearly defined and described. On the far left, the armed warrior is tilted slightly backwards, as if he was caught in surprise by the tiger turning back and roaring at him, either intentional or accidental. This small detail adds much intrigue to this image.

A 面

砖画印像：加拿大皇家安大略博物馆藏洛阳出土西汉画像空心砖

Impressions on Clay: Pictorial Hollow-Brick Tomb Tiles From Western Han Luoyang (2ⁿᵈ century BC)

持戟武士骏马凤鸟砖

◎ 长 119 厘米　高 47 厘米　厚 15.5 厘米

◎ 怀履光收藏，ROM 编号 931.13.276

Tomb Tile Depicting Armed Warriors, Horse, and Phoenix

Length: 119 cm; Height: 47 cm; Thickness: 15.5 cm

Bishop William C. White Collection, 931.13.276

两面画像种类相同。砖面上有持戟佩剑武士（Ⅰ型）、长尾凤鸟（Ⅶ型）和马（Ⅷ型）。持戟佩剑武士与前页砖上的相同。A面上有朱书『和下』二字，字的方向与画像上下相反。

边纹是带点菱纹。

B面

The composition of the picture on this tile is similar to that on the tile 931.13.133, but short of the tree. Two characters are brushed on the surface in cinnabar, " 和下 " read as "and，lower," but in a reversed orientation of the pictorial elements. The character "和" or *he* (or and) may also interpreted here as "joint," indicating a recommendation for two tiles joining at a lower row.

朱书文字

武士骏马凤鸟砖

◎ 长 146 厘米　高 48 厘米　厚 15.5 厘米

◎ 怀履光收藏，编号 931.13.269

Tomb Tile Depicting Warriors, Horses, and Phoenixes

Length: 146 cm; Height: 48 cm; Thickness: 15.5 cm

Bishop William C. White Collection, 931.13.269

A 面

B 面

两面画像种类和印制情况相同。上有佩剑武士、长尾凤鸟（Ⅶ型）和马（Ⅶ型），右边有近三分之一的砖面是空白。佩剑武士与前页砖上持戟佩剑武士是同模印制，但是武士的小臂、双手、剑柄和长戟部分印得非常轻浅，几不可见，推测可能是印模出现问题。A 面有朱书『东南上』三字，字的方向与画像上下相反。

边纹是菱格纹，印模长 11.4 厘米，宽 7.5 厘米。

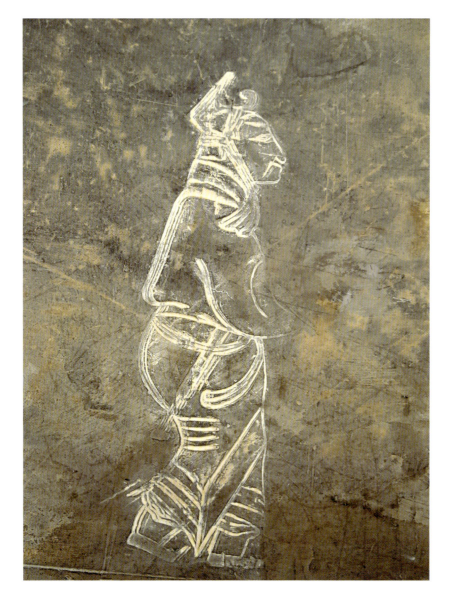

On this tile, images of warriors armed with swords alternate with images of neighing horses and long-tailed phoenixes. Missing parts of the stamped images on this tile indicate possible human error and/or technical difficulties in the production process.

On one side (or Side A) of this tile, three characters appear in cinnabar, " 东南上 " that read as "east, south, upper" or as a phrase "southeast upper." The characters were written in a reversed orientation of the pictorial elements.

朱书文字

端面

持戟武士骏马虎凤鸟鹤砖

◎ 长 171 厘米　高 47.5 厘米　厚 16.7 厘米

◎ 怀履光收藏，ROM 编印为 931.13.272

Tomb Tile Depicting Armed Warriors, Tree, Horse, Tiger, Phoenix, and Crane

Length: 171 cm; Height: 47.5 cm; Thickness: 16.7 cm

Bishop William C. White Collection, 931.13.272

B 面

A 面

两面画像种类和排布有差别。A面上有持戟佩剑武士（II型）、马（VII型）、鹤（I型）、树木（II型）、虎（II型）和短尾凤鸟（II型）。持戟佩剑武士，与I型武士相似，但面左，两者显然不是出自同一个印模。短尾凤鸟面右。多个画像有印模边框的痕迹。有朱书『口下』二字。B面没有鹤。

边纹是菱格纹，印模长10.8厘米，宽6.2—6.5厘米。

This is another warrior theme with horse, tiger, tree, and an auspicious bird. Pictures on the two sides are of similar design with variations in individual elements; one side (Side B) is also short of a shrieking crane. The warrior is armed with a halberd and a short sword, apparently the same design as that of the tile 931.13.276, but facing the opposite direction, suggesting that the same drawing was used to make different stamps.

On one side (Side A) of this tile, two characters appear in cinnabar red, " □下 " read as "?, lower," with the first character unreadable.

A 面

持戟武士骏马凤鸟鹤砖

◎ 长 142 厘米　高 52 厘米　厚 15 厘米

◎ 怀履光收藏，ROM 编号为 931.13.1.29

Tomb Tile Depicting an Armed Warrior, Tree, Horse, Phoenix, and Crane

Length: 142 cm; Height: 52 cm; Thickness: 15 cm
Bishop William C. White Collection, 931.13.129

两面画像种类相同，唯排列顺序有差别。砖面上有短尾凤鸟（II型）、鹤（I型）、马（VII型）、持戟佩剑武士（II型）和树木（II型）。A面有『西北上』三字，字的方向与画像上下相反。B面武士的戟头左侧有弧形印模边框痕迹。

边纹是菱格纹，印模长10.5厘米，宽6.5厘米。

    Similar composition to that on tile 931.13.272, but short of the tiger. On one side (Side B), the warrior's halberd shows a rounded edge of the wooden stamp.

    On one side (Side A) of this tile, three characters painted in cinnabar, " 西 北上 " that read as "west, north, upper" or as a phrase "northwest upper. " The characters were written in a reversed orientation of the pictorial elements.

持戈武士天马凤鸟砖

长132厘米　高53厘米　厚15厘米

怀履光收藏，ROM编号为931.13.130

Tomb Tile Depicting Warriors Armed with Dagger-Axe, Winged Horses, and Phoenixes

Length: 132 cm; Height: 53 cm; Thickness: 15 cm

Bishop William C. White Collection, 931.13.130

砖画印像：加拿大皇家安大略博物馆藏洛阳出土西汉画像空心砖

Impressions on Clay: Pictorial Hollow-Brick Tomb Tiles From Western Han Luoyang (2ⁿᵈ century BC)

A 面

两面画像种类相同，排布有差别。砖面上层是两只长尾凤鸟（Ⅵ型），下层是持戈武士（Ⅰ型）和天马（Ⅰ型）。天马的体形壮硕浑实，身上装饰翼形和云形的花纹。凤鸟画像模印不全。A 面上有朱书『南上』二字。B 面画像模印轻浅。

边纹是菱格纹，模长 11.5 厘米，宽 7.2 厘米。

B 面

The picture of warrior, horse, and phoenix on this tile is in the same manner to the other warrior themed compositions, in a similar "land and sky" horizontal spatial arrangement. The warrior figure is the same as the one on the tile 931.13.124; the horse is rendered in a fascinatingly decorative manner, with geometric treatment of parts of its body, and an abstract cloud pattern accompanying its elegant wing.

On one side (or Side A) of this tile, two characters painted in cinnabar, " 南上 " read as "south, upper" to indicate a location of "south upper."

A 面

持戈武士骏马虎凤鸟砖

◎ 长 149 厘米　高 51 厘米　厚 14.5 厘米

◎ 怀履光收藏，ROM 编号为 931.13.268

Tomb Tile Depicting Warrior Armed with Dagger-Axe, Horse, Tiger, and Phoenix

Length: 149 cm; Height: 51 cm; Thickness: 14.5 cm

Bishop William C. White Collection, 931.13.268

砖画印像：加拿大皇家安大略博物馆藏洛阳出土西汉画像空心砖

Impressions on Clay: Pictorial Hollow-Brick Tomb Tiles From Western Han Luoyang (2nd century BC)

280

两面画像种类相同，排布有差别。上层是三只凤鸟（Ⅳ型），下层是执戈武士（Ⅰ型）、马（Ⅰ型）和虎（Ⅲ型）。A面有朱书『西□』二字。边纹是菱格纹。上侧面有两条菱格纹。

The composition on this tile is similar to the tile 931.13.130, but with a tiger added to the scene, some titillating tension is created in the dynamics of the image. The implicit interaction between the figures and the hidden narrative now have an element of surprise and mystery. The horse is also of another model, identical to that of the tile 931.13.120.

On one side (or Side A) of this tile, there are two handwritten characters in cinnabar "西□" read as "west, ?" with the second character unrecognizable.

A 面

持戈武士骏马虎凤鸟砖

Tomb Tile Depicting Warrior Armed with Dagger-Axe, Horse, Tiger, and Phoenix

◎ 长 130 厘米　高 47 厘米　厚 14.5 厘米

◎ 怀履光收藏，ROM 编号为 931.13.385

Length: 130 cm; Height: 47 cm; Thickness: 14.5 cm
Bishop William C. White Collection, 931.13.385

两面画像略有不同。A面有执戈武士（I型）、长尾凤鸟（IV型）、虎（I型）和马（II型）。B面没有虎，凤鸟上下颠倒了。画像印得比较浅，不甚清晰，马和凤鸟都有重影现象。边纹为菱格纹。

B面

The design and pictorial elements are similar to the tile 931.13.268, but the impression of the stamped images is left quite light. Composition on one side is short of the tiger, and the phoenix is upside-down. It may compromise the pictorial coherence of the design, but errors such as this is quite valuable to understand the making of these images.

持戈武士骏马虎凤鸟砖

◎ 长 121 厘米　高 47 厘米　厚 15.5 厘米

◎ 怀履光收藏，编号为 931.13.125

Tomb Tile Depicting Warrior, Horse, Tiger, and Phoenix

Length: 121 cm; Height: 47 cm; Thickness: 15.5 cm

Bishop William C. White Collection, 931.13.125

两面画像种类和排布相同。上层有两只长尾凤鸟（Ⅳ型），下层有执戈武士（Ⅰ型）、虎（Ⅰ型）和马（Ⅳ型）。A面有朱书『东北上』三字。砖上四位武士画像上有一条纵贯全身的断开线。其中，A面右侧武士画像的线条不仅断开，而且严重错位。两匹马画像上有一条横穿马腿的断开线。凤鸟画像上也有同样的断开线。

边纹为菱格纹，印模长11厘米，宽5.7厘米。

A面

B面

砖画印像··加拿大皇家安大略博物馆藏洛阳出土西汉画像空心砖

Impressions on Clay: Pictorial Hollow-Brick Tomb Tiles From Western Han Luoyang (2nd century BC)

This picture contains figures of warrior, tiger, horse, and phoenix, again grouped into two spatial divisions: the ground and the sky. This tile is one of the six tiles that share a similar design, composed with similar pictorial elements, suggesting that perhaps they were the result of a "mass production," made as one group, at the same workshop. That assumption is coherent to the handwriting on the surface of the tile indicating where the tile should be placed after being transported from the workshop to the burial site.

On one side (or Side A) of this tile, three characters painted in cinnabar, " 东北上 " that read as "east, north, upper" or as a phrase "northeast upper."

持戈武士骏马虎凤鸟砖

◎ 长 136 厘米　高 47 厘米　厚 15.5 厘米

◎ 怀履光收藏，ROM 编号尺 931.13.265

Tomb Tile Depicting Warrior, Horse, Tiger, and Phoenix

Length: 136 cm; Height: 47 cm; Thickness: 15.5 cm

Bishop William C. White Collection, 931.13.265

B 面

A 面

画像与前页砖基本一样。A 面有朱书『东南上』
三字。B 面武士、马和凤鸟画像都有断开线，马
画像的断开线错位明显。

The pictorial image is almost identical with that of the tile 931.13.125, again possibly made from the same workshop. The warrior, horse, and phoenix figures on one site (Side B) all show disruption in the linework, indicating that the wooden stamps were not as carefully aligned during the stamping process.

On one side (or Side A) of this tile, three characters painted in cinnabar, " 东南上 " that read as "east, south, upper" or as a phrase "southeast upper. "

A 面

持戈武士骏马虎凤鸟砖

长 120 厘米　高 47.5 厘米　厚 16 厘米
怀履光收藏，ROM 编号为 931.13.386

Tomb Tile Depicting Warrior, Horse, Tiger, and Phoenix

Length: 120 cm; Height: 47.5 cm; Thickness: 16 cm
Bishop William C. White Collection, 931.13.386

画像与前页砖基本一样。A面有朱书『和上』二字。画像上的断开线不明显。

B 面

The pictorial figures are identical with that of the tile 931.13.125. Two characters brushed with cinnabar on one side are the same seen on the tile 931.13.276: " 和上 " read as "and, upper." The character 和 or *he* (or and) may also be interpreted here as "joint," indicating a recommendation for two tiles joining at an upper row.

Tomb Tile Depicting Warrior, Horse, Tiger, and Phoenix

Length: 135 cm; Height: 48 cm; Thickness: 15.5 cm
Bishop William C. White Collection, 931.13.270

长 135 厘米　高 48 厘米　厚 15.5 厘米

怀履光收藏，ROM 编号为 931.13.270

A 面

砖上画像和边纹与前页砖基本一样。Ａ面有朱书痕迹，文字无法辨识。

The picture and decorative borders of this tile are almost identical with that of the tile 931.13.125. There are still traces of cinnabar handwriting, but character(s) could not be recognized.

持戈武士骏马虎凤鸟砖

怀履光收藏，ROM 编号为 931.13.260

长 135 厘米　高 48 厘米　厚 15.5 厘米

Tomb Tile Depicting Warrior, Horse, Tiger, and Phoenix

Length: 135 cm; Height: 48 cm; Thickness: 15.5 cm
Bishop William C. White Collection, 931.13.260

A 面

砖上画像和边纹与前页砖基本一样。画像模印轻浅，不甚清晰。A 面有朱书『西（南？）上』三字。B 面只有一名武士像。

砖画印像：加拿大皇家安大略博物馆藏洛阳出土西汉画像空心砖

Impressions on Clay: Pictorial Hollow-Brick Tomb Tiles From Western Han Luoyang (2nd century BC)

B 面

The picture and decorative borders of this tile are almost identical with that of the tile 931.13.125, although the pictorial image is stamped very lightly, leaving a blurred impression. Image on the back side (Side B) contains only one warrior.

Three characters were written in cinnabar brushed on one side (Side A): " 西（南 ?）上 " that read as "west, (south?), upper" or as a phrase "southwest(?) upper. "

持戈武士骏马虎凤鸟砖

长 134.5 厘米　高 48 厘米　厚 15.5 厘米

怀履光收藏，ROM 编号为 931.13.267

Tomb Tile Depicting Warrior, Horse, Tiger, and Phoenix

Length: 134.5 cm; Height: 48 cm; Thickness: 15.5 cm

Bishop William C. White Collection, 931.13.267

A 面

砖上画像和边纹与前页砖基本一样。A 面有朱书字迹，难以辨识。B 面没有马画像。边纹为菱格纹。

B 面

The picture and decorative borders of this tile are almost identical with that of the tile 931.13.125. Composition on the back side (Side B) is absent of horses, and the images are very lightly stamped. Traces of handwriting on Side A can be seen, but the characters could not be deciphered.

持戈武士骏马虎砖

长 121 厘米　高 47.5 厘米　厚 15.5 厘米

怀履光收藏，ROM 编号 931.13.271

Tomb Tile Depicting Warrior with Dagger-Axe, Horse, and Tiger

Length: 121 cm; Height: 47.5 cm; Thickness: 15.5 cm
Bishop William C. White Collection, 931.13.271

A 面

两面画像种类相同。有虎（I 型）、马（IV 型）和执戈武士（I 型）三个画像，一字排开，画像模印轻浅。A 面有朱书『上和』二字。边纹是菱格纹。

On this tile, figures of a tiger, a horse, and a warrior are spread evenly across the picture plane. Two characters brushed onto the surface with cinnabar are clearly visible: " 上和 " read as "upper, and" similar to that on tiles 931.13.276 and 931.13.386.

持戟武士骏马虎凤鸟砖

Tomb Tile Depicting Warrior with Halberd, Horse, Tiger, and Phoenix

长 123 厘米　高 47.5 厘米　厚 14.5 厘米

怀履光收藏，ROM 编号 931.13.11

Length: 123 cm; Height: 47.5 cm; Thickness: 14.5 cm
Bishop William C. White Collection, 931.13.11

A 面

两面画像种类相同，排布顺序有差别。上有持戟武士（Ⅰ型）、马（Ⅳ型）、虎（Ⅰ型）和长尾凤鸟（Ⅳ型）、短尾凤鸟（Ⅰ型）。A 面有朱书字迹，难以辨识。边纹是菱格纹，印模长 11.5 厘米，宽 7.2 厘米。

B 面

Images on this tile appear to be severely abrased or lightly stamped. The composition consists of a tiger, two horses, a warrior armed with halberd and sword in the foreground, and a row of phoenixes of short tails and long tails in the sky. Traces of handwriting on Side A can be seen, but the characters could not be deciphered.

Appendices

附 录

附录一：画像砖图案分解统计

一、画像类别

1、人物画像

名称	型式	画像	尺寸（厘米）	特征	砖号
持戈武士	I		高27.3 宽15	头戴冠，冠颊、缨、垂缕刻画细致清晰；颈部有护领；身穿宽袖长襦大袴，腰间束带，带上有纹绣；脚穿卷头履。手持长戈。	124 125 386 265 270 260 267 385 268 130 271
持戈武士	II		高25.7 宽12.2	头戴冠，冠的前部有一向上翻卷的突起，冠颊、缨、垂缕刻画细致清晰；身穿宽袖前长后短的长襦，腰束有纹绣的宽带；脚穿卷头履。手持长戈，腰间佩剑。剑鞘细长，末端镶有剑摽。	123
持戟武士	I		高23.8 宽11	头戴冠，冠的前部有一向上翻卷的突起，冠颊、缨、垂缕刻画细致清晰；身穿长襦，腰间除了腰带另系一根剑带，剑带结系后长出的部分飘垂身侧；足穿絇履。右手持戟，腰间佩剑。佩剑通过剑璏悬挂在剑带上。	133 269 276 11
持戟武士	II		高23.4 宽10	装束同I型持戟武士。	129 272

名称	型式	画像	尺寸（厘米）	特征	砖号
持杖武士	I		高 24.8 宽 10.5	戴尖角状的冠，冠前有向上卷翘的突起，冠缨很长，结系后垂缕飘至肩后；身穿长襦大袴，长襦前后襟稍长，侧襟略短；足穿绚履。腰间悬挂短剑，左手持上端饰有一物的长杖。	138 139 259
弓箭手	I		高 21.2 宽 17	束发插簪；身着袖口和袴管口有纹绣的短襦短袴、足穿绚履，呈跪蹲状，上身反转，张弓射箭。	131 132 142.A 142.B
佩剑武士	I		高 28 剑长 24	头戴冠，身穿长襦大袴，足穿绚履。腰间除了腰带另系一根剑带，长剑悬挂于剑带上。为便于活动，长襦的前后襟剪成三角形。	134
佩剑武士	II		高 21.5 宽 18	头戴巾，着深衣，足穿绚履。腰悬长剑，躬身抱拳施礼。	137
士族	I		高 20.9 宽 10.5	头戴冠，着深衣，足穿绚履。身体微躬，抱拳施礼。	137
士族	II		高 27.7 宽 8.3	头戴冠，着宽袖深衣，足穿绚履。颌下生须。	137

名称	型式	画像	尺寸（厘米）	特征	砖号
儒生			高 27 宽 9.5	头戴巾，着宽袖深衣，足穿絢履。手持一册竹书。	137
驯马人			高 22.5 宽 16	束发插簪；身着交领长襦，领口、袖口有纹绣；腰束带，下着袴；足穿絢履。手握缰绳。	131
彀骑			高 10.9 宽 16.5	头戴鹖冠，身穿窄袖短襦，腰间束带，下穿大袴，背负箭箙。上身反转，张弓欲射。马做飞奔疾驰之状。马鬃修剪整齐，辔头齐全，马背上的鞍垫用肚带绑缚，鞍垫前后有装饰物，无马镫。	121 122 273
胡彀骑			高 21.5 宽 34.4	头戴尖帽，身穿交领左衽短襦，下穿袴。两腿弯曲紧夹马身，双手张弓欲射。乘马头部前伸，四蹄奋起呈疾驰之状。马有辔头、鞍垫，无马镫。鞍垫通过胸带、肚带和鞦带固定在马背上。	143.A 143.B
骑吏			高 17.2 宽 26.8	头戴武弁，上穿宽袖襦，下着大袴，手握缰绳。马呈疾驰之状，辔头齐全，马镫清晰。马鬃和骑吏的衣袖向后飘扬。	128

2、马画像

名称	型式	画像	尺寸（厘米）	特征	砖号
骏马	I		高 18.5 宽 23	头戴辔头。马鬃经过修剪。	268
	II		高 17.9 宽 27.3	头戴辔头。无鬃。	261 385
	III		高 17.9 宽 27.5	头戴辔头。马鬃经过修剪。腹部有装饰花纹。	127
	IV		高 21 宽 23	马鬃经过修剪。	264 126 125 120 133 132 11 386 265 271 270 260 267
	V		高 22.5 宽 27.8	头戴辔头。马鬃和缰绳均是画像印好后刻划的。	131
	VI		高 20.5 宽 27.6	马头与辔头与 V 型骏马略有差别。后颈部位线条加粗以表示马鬃。	133
	VII		高 19.2 宽 22.8	马鬃经过修剪。	276 272 269 129

名称	型式	画像	尺寸（厘米）	特征	砖号
骏马	VIII		高 19.7 宽 22	马鬃经过修剪。马鬃和马尾部分与 VII 型骏马略有差别。	266　184 185
	IX X		左： 高 3.8 宽 4.9 右： 高 5.8 宽 5.3		184 185 266
天马	I		高 21 宽 20.5	体形壮硕浑实，大耳，马背上拱，身上有涡形、翼形和云形花纹，短尾。	130　183 263　375 182
	II		高 18.4 宽 17.5	头部细长，腮部壮大夸张，颈部有修剪齐整的马鬃。	136
	III		高 18.8 宽 18	与 II 型天马相似，但无鬃，靠近腹部后腿处的花纹也有差别。	134 135
	IV		高 27.2 宽 26	短脸大眼，腮部硕大，脖子颀长，无鬃。身体饱满浑实，有翼，小尾，马腿与写实型的骏马相比显得短小。马蹄尤其特别，类兽。	139 259
	V		高 18.8 宽 19	头部细长，眼睛滚圆，腮部硕大夸张，饰有三个圆圈。身体浑实饱满，马腿肌肉雄壮。	136　40.1

3、凤鸟画像

名称	型式	画像	尺寸（厘米）	特征	砖号
长尾凤鸟	I		高 15.7 宽 19.5	面左，鸡冠，长翅略收。	131
	II		高 14.8 宽 23	面左，半圆冠，长翅，一翅平展。	127
	III		高 11.3 宽 13	面左，鸡冠，短翅略收。	266 184 185
	IV		高 14 宽 19.5	面右。	125 265 385 268 386 270 267 260 11
	V		高 13.4 宽 18.5	面右。	128 261
	VI		高 8.6 宽 12.3	面右。	130
	VII		高 12 宽 11	面右。	276 269

名称	型式	画像	尺寸 （厘米）	特征	砖号
长尾凤鸟	Ⅷ		高 12 宽 9.7	面右。	138 139 259
短尾凤鸟	Ⅰ		高 10.9 宽 10.4	面左。	132　133 142.A 142.B 11
	Ⅱ		高 11.5 宽 10	面右。	272　183 357　263 182　129
	Ⅲ		高 10 宽 9.4	面左，口衔瑞珠。	120
	Ⅳ		高 10.5 宽 9.2	面右，口衔瑞珠。	135

4、龙画像

名称	画像	尺寸（厘米）	特征	砖号
飞龙		高 39 宽 81.5	身躯呈波浪起伏之状，上面饰有圆圈和曲折的双线；角似牛角，鹰爪。	118 186
武士御龙		高 36 宽 88	身躯呈波浪起伏之状，上面饰有圆圈和曲折的双线；龙角是角尖呈螺旋状的长角，鹰爪。武士身着交领左衽短襦、短袴，呈半跪姿势，右手持盾，左手挥舞短剑。	118 186

5、虎画像

型式	画像	尺寸（厘米）	特征	砖号
I		高 11 宽 19.4	作驻足回首张望状，身上的条纹是 S 形双钩波磔纹。	266 184 185 386 385 11 125 265 270 267 271 133 142.A
II		高 11.1 宽 18.6	同 I 型虎，面向相反。	272 264
III		高 16 宽 24	作驻足回首张望状，身上有平行的斜线和折角线状的条纹，颈上有项圈。	268 128 263 182
IV		高 9.6 宽 17.8	作驻足回首张望状，身上有双线条纹。	127
V		高 9.3 宽 19.6	前腿抬起，作踏步行走状，身上的条纹是 S 形双钩波磔纹，腹部有三个星纹。	121 122 273
VI		高 6.5 宽 18.1	向前奔跃，身上的条纹有平行的曲线和 S 形线条。	119

6、鹤画像

型式	画像	尺寸（厘米）	砖号
I		高 13.2 宽 7	129 272
II		高 10.8 宽 8	261
III		高 11.2 宽 6.7	136 137
IV		高 10 宽 6.3	136

7、雁画像

型式	画像	尺寸（厘米）	砖号
I		高 5.8 宽 13	136 117 137 140 141
II		高 9.4 宽 7.5	136 137 40.1
III		高 7 宽 13.5	117 140 141
IV		高 7.2 宽 13	134

8、鹿画像

型式	画像	尺寸（厘米）	砖号
I		高 11.2 宽 17.1	143.A 143.B 136 140 141 117
II		高 17 宽 25.7	142.A 142.B 126 131
III		高 8.7 宽 17	119

9、树木画像

型式	画像	尺寸 （厘米）	砖号
I		高 35.5 宽 16.8	266　184 185　136 137
II		高 26.3 宽 13.4	272　129
III		高约 38.5 宽 14.5	134 40.1
IV		高 23 宽 11.2	131　133

10、鹰隼画像

型式	画像	尺寸 （厘米）	砖号
I		高 11.5 宽 12.6	131
II		高 11.6 宽 12.1	131

11、朱鹭画像

型式	画像	尺寸（厘米）	特征	砖号
Ⅰ Ⅱ		左侧 高 7.2 宽 2.8 中间 高 6.9 宽 3.9	三只朱鹭刻在一块印模上，朱鹭有两种造型。	122

12、其他画像

名称	画像	尺寸（厘米）	特征	砖号
猎豹		高 9.2 宽 16	身上有斑点。	142.B 131　126
猎犬		高 8.8 宽 18.2	颈带项圈，神色机警。	141　140 117　135 136　137
兔		高 3.9 宽 7.9		135　136
鹜		高 6.1 宽 11.8		134
猴		高 4.2 宽 2.7	面右，蹲坐状。	134　40.1

二、几何纹饰

1、边缘纹饰

名称	型式	图样	尺寸（厘米）	砖号
菱格纹	I		长 12.2 高 6	121
	II		长 12.3 高 8.1	135
	III		长 8.8 高 4.2	126 B面
	IV		长 10 高 4	131 A面
	V		长 24 高 2.8	138
勾连云纹	I		长 10.5 高 4.3	138 139 259
	II		长 8.6 高 4.2	121
	III		长 27.5—29 高 4.7	131 B面
弈纹			长 6.8 高 8.5	135

名称	型式	图样	尺寸（厘米）	砖号
嘉禾纹	I		底长 3.3 高 2.4	121
	II		底长 4.7 高 2.6	40.1
	III		底长 4.5 高 2.3	134
	IV		底长 3.5 高 2.5	139
勾连云纹双结纹			长 11.6 高 6	119
瑞草纹			长 11.5 高 4.4	119
斜线纹				259

2、侧面纹饰

名称	纹饰	砖号
四叶纹		143.A 143.B
菱格纹		142.A 142.B 123 263 182 118 135
勾连云纹 变形菱格纹		140 141 117 136 137
斜线纹 4S 方格纹		40.1
勾连云纹 柿蒂纹		131 132 126 134
斜线纹 变形菱格纹		186
勾连云纹 4S 方格纹		134
勾连云纹 双结纹 星纹		119

三、文字

内容	书写方式	砖号	排列方式
西北上	朱书	129	上中下一列
西北下	朱书	132	上中下一列
		183	左一右二两列
西南上	朱书	266	左二右一两列
西（南？）上		260	一行
东北上	朱书	182	左二右一两列
		125	左一右二两列
东北下	朱书	184	一行
东南上	朱书	185	左二右一两列
		269	一行
		265	左一右二两列
和上	朱书	386	上下
上和	朱书	271	上下
和下	朱书	276	上下
东（南？）	朱书	126	上下
西□	朱书	268	一行
□下	朱书	272	一行
北下	朱书	261	一行
南上	朱书	130	上下
上	朱书	131	
南和西	刻划	186	上中下一列
无法辨识	朱书	270 267 11	

见微知著

——洛阳西汉阴纹画像空心砖模印技术的痕迹研究

徐婵菲　［加拿大］沈　辰

　　自西汉起始，出现了一种新的墓葬类型，即画像砖墓。用于建墓的各类形制的砖中有一部分是上面装饰有人物、动物和植物等画像的砖，考古学上将这种砖称作汉画像砖。画像的制作方法有模制、笔绘、刻划和雕塑等几种，其中最常用的是模制法。

　　所谓模制法，就是先制作画像的木质印模，然后用印模在湿软的泥坯上像盖图章一样印出画像的方法。汉代墓砖上的画像大多数是用印模印制的，所以，印模对汉画像砖的意义自不待言。那么，画像印模是什么样子？又是如何印制画像呢？历史文献上没有关于汉砖画像印模及模印技术的记载，对它的研究只能借助于实物资料。在此，我们通过洛阳出土的西汉阴纹画像空心砖［图一：1—4］资料来探讨一下这个问题。我们之所以选择洛阳西汉阴纹画像空心砖，原因主要有：一是特征明显，极易辨别，实物资料丰富；二是出现时间早，画像艺术水平高，制作技术成熟；三是画像为阴纹，而且尺幅有大有小，富于变化，印模在制作和使用方面工艺复杂，技术难度高。因此，弄清楚洛阳汉砖画像印模及模印技术对于解决其他地区的同类问题大有帮助。

　　洛阳西汉阴纹画像空心砖的特征正如其名所示，砖型是体量宏大、内部空虚的空心砖。画像空心砖有长方形和三角形两种：长方形砖，长90—

[图一] 洛阳西汉阴纹画像空心砖：

[图一：1] 加拿大皇家安大略博物馆藏洛阳出土西汉阴纹画像空心砖（底长 85 厘米、高 90 厘米、厚 15 厘米）

[图一：2] 加拿大皇家安大略博物馆藏洛阳出土西汉阴纹画像空心砖（长 165.5 厘米、高 53 厘米、厚 17 厘米）

[图一：3] 故宫博物院藏洛阳出土西汉阴纹画像空心砖（长 164.8 厘米、高 51.4 厘米），采自《故宫雕塑馆》页 142，故宫出版社，2015 年。

[图一：4] 洛阳市宜阳牌窑西汉墓出土彩绘画像砖（长 180 厘米、高 54 厘米、厚 18 厘米）

180 厘米，宽 40—65 厘米，厚 14—18 厘米；三角形砖，底长 81—108 厘米，高 80—91 厘米，厚 15—18 厘米。砖上画像是阴纹画像，即构成画像的线条是低于砖面的阴纹线条，这是洛阳西汉画像空心砖最显著的特征。

洛阳西汉阴纹画像空心砖大量出土于 20 世纪 30 年代前后，流布甚广，国内外许多博物馆都有收藏。在广泛收集资料的基础上，我们对收藏于加拿大皇家安大略博物馆、美国尼尔森—阿特金斯博物馆及中国故宫博物院、洛阳古代艺术博物馆、洛阳市文物考古研究院、宜阳县文物保护管理所和郑州市华夏文化艺术博物馆的 160 余块洛阳西汉阴纹画像空心砖做了仔细的观察，通过分析、研究画像上存在的各种现象，对画像印模和模印技术有了一些新的看法，撰文陈述，以与同好者商讨。

一、观察对象

洛阳西汉阴纹画像空心砖通常有六个面，正反两个大面、上下两个侧面和左右两个端面。画像一般位于两个大面上，大多数砖两面的画像是一样的。砖上画像的数量有少有多，少者一个（如龙纹画像砖），多者有四十多个（如猎犬猎雁砖）。无论砖上有多少个画像，它们都是工匠用印模按预先设计好的位置一个一个印上去的。印模可以反复使用，所以同一个画像会反复出现在砖上。据统计，出现在洛阳西汉阴纹画像空心砖上的画像种类有 18 种，样式超过 90 个，就是说工匠需要制作出数量超过 90 个的印模才能完成洛阳汉砖画像的制作工作。但截至目前，考古发掘中没有发现一件与砖上画像相同的金属或陶质的印模实物，有机质制作的印模因易腐难以保存下来。所以一直以来，研究洛阳汉砖画像的学者都认为画像印模是木质的[1]。

根据研究，砖上画像的制作极有可能为如下流程：首先，雕刻木质阳纹印模；其次，工匠根据"设计蓝本"从一堆印模中选出要用的印模，然

1　怀履光是第一个提出洛阳汉砖画像印模为木质的学者（[加拿大]怀履光著，徐婵菲译、[加拿大]沈辰校：《中国（洛阳）古墓砖图考》，中州古籍出版社，2014 年，第 27 页），后来许多学者认同这一说法（黄明兰：《洛阳汉画像砖》，河南美术出版社，1986 年，第 6 页；吕品：《河南汉代画像砖的出土与研究》，《中原文物》1989 年第 3 期，第 51—59 页）。

［图二］阴纹画像的制作流程（Rose Ting-yi Liu 绘图）：

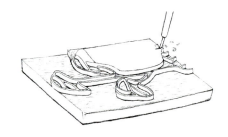

［图二：1］雕刻木质阳纹印模

［图二：2］根据"设计蓝本"选出印模

［图二：3］模印画像

［图二：4］模印完成

后，看清印模的方向（避免印出颠倒、歪斜的画像）、确定模印的位置；最后，用合适的力度和角度按下印模［图二：1—4］。印好一个画像，再以同样的程序模印下一个画像，再下一个，诸如此类。但工匠不是机器，人工操作容易受到各种客观因素（泥坯干湿软硬、印模质量等）和主观因素（工匠技术水平、工作时的状态等）的影响，这一系列动作在一定时间内不断地重复，难免出现差错，使一些不该有的现象出现在画像上或者砖上。所谓不该有的现象，是指画像深浅不一［图三］，重影［图四］，歪斜甚至上下颠倒，画像中的某些线条出现断开、错位［图五］，画像周边有印模边框的痕迹等。我们将存在有上述一种或者几种现象的画像称为"问题画像"。我们的

［图三］深浅不一的画像

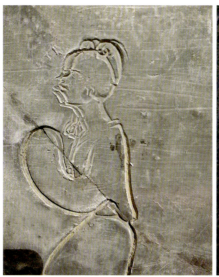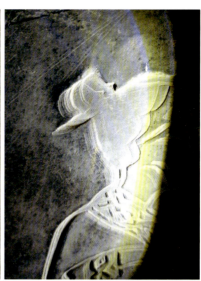

[图四] 重影的画像

[图五] 线条断开及错位的画像

观察对象正是这些因工匠"疏忽"制造出来的"问题画像"，它们为探究画像印模的形制和画像的模印技术提供了痕迹研究线索。我们对这些平时不太关注的问题画像做痕迹研究的目的，是希望复原印模的形状、印模的结构，以及印模本身的图像。本文在此观察的基础上，对西汉洛阳地区阳纹印模（对应画像砖的阴纹画像）的特征，以及其产生的"问题"画像做出推断和分析。

[图六] 留下印模边框痕迹的画像

[图六：1] 加拿大皇家安大略博物馆藏（长 122 厘米、高 53 厘米、厚 15 厘米；凤鸟画像长 9.7 厘米、高 12 厘米，印模长 10.6 厘米、高 15.3 厘米）

[图六：2] 凤鸟画像印模边框痕迹

二、画像印模

1. 印模的形状

工匠用印模往泥坯上印制画像，按压力度和角度恰到好处时，印出的画像清晰、均匀，低于阳纹画像的印模边框不会出现在砖上。如果用力过大，不仅画像会"深陷"泥中，印模边框也会或多或少地触及泥面，留下印迹。通过这些印迹，可以了解印模的形状。

如[图六：1]是收藏于加拿大皇家安大略博物馆的画像砖[2]，砖上的四只凤鸟画像周围或多或少留下了印模边框的痕迹，在上层左边那只凤鸟的上方、下方和左侧三面都有印模边框的痕迹。根据上层右边那只凤鸟下方的痕迹，可以确定这只凤鸟画像印模的形状是长方形。[图六：2]印模左下角受力大，致使印模边框深深印在泥坯里。图七猎犬画像的左侧留下印模边框的痕迹，因缺少其它三面的资料，故猎犬印模形状不明。图八为洛阳市文物考古研究院藏砖上的虎画像及印模边框痕迹，从现有痕迹来看，印模形状可能是长方形。图九在彀骑画像的上方、左下方和右侧数处留下不连贯的印模边框痕迹，从现有痕迹来看，印模形状与彀骑轮廓近似，为不规则形。图十为洛阳市文物考古研究院藏砖上的马画像，从马耳部位、马背上方和马尾后方的印模边框痕迹看，这块马画像印模的形状也是不规则形，若以马身体为水平方向，那么这块印模极不端正。图十一为郑州市华夏文化艺术

2　下文所用材料与图片，如不注明，则均来自加拿大皇家安大略博物馆。

[图七]猎犬画像及印模边框痕迹（猎犬画像长18.2厘米、高8.8厘米，印模高9厘米）　[图八]洛阳市文物考古研究院藏砖上的虎画像及印模边框痕迹

[图九]毂骑画像及印模边框痕迹　[图十]洛阳市文物考古研究院藏砖上的马画像及印模边框痕迹

[图十一]郑州市华夏文化艺术博物馆藏砖上的鹤与凤鸟画像　[图十二]执戟武士戟头左上方弧形印模边框痕迹　[图十三]日本天理参考馆藏砖上的马画像

博物馆藏砖上的鹤与凤鸟画像，据观察，凤鸟画像先印，后被鹤画像叠压，画像上方留下的半个梯形印模边框应是鹤画像印模的上半部分，印模下半部分的形状不明。图十二持戟武士画像戟头左上方的那条弧线应是印模边框的痕迹。图十三为日本天理大学古物馆藏砖上马画像，画像左右深浅不一，右侧马首和右前腿很深，但未在马首和右前腿周围见到印模边框痕迹，可确定马首和右前腿阳纹外轮廓线就是印模边框[3]。

3　天理大学、天理教道友社：《天理大学附属天理参考馆藏品》，[日本]天理教道友社，昭和61年（1986），第134页。

［图十四］加拿大皇家安大略博物馆藏（长143厘米、高54.3厘米、厚17.5厘米）

　　从上面实例可以看出，洛阳汉砖的画像印模的形状多种多样，有的规则，有的不规则，通常与画像的形状近似，印模的大小也与画像差不多。这样设计的目的是尽量减小印模面积，便于工匠在印制画像时控制画像之间的距离与高低。但这种设计的弊病也很明显，想用那些形状既不规则又不端正的印模印出百分之百的"正品"画像是有难度的，所以砖上出现"马失前蹄"［图十四］"上下颠倒"的画像在所难免。

　　2.印模的结构

　　虽未发现汉砖画像印模实物，我们可以参考时代与之相近的其他材质的印模实物来推知汉砖画像印模的结构。

　　1983年，在广州西汉南越王墓出土两件用于丝织物印花的青铜印花凸版[4]。两件花版一大一小，形状不同，花纹各异，但结构一样，主体是一个扁薄的铜板，铜板正面是凸起的线状花纹，背面有一个带穿的小钮［图十五:1—

［图十五］广州西汉南越王墓出土的青铜印花凸版：

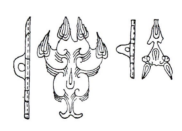

［图十五:1］青铜印花凸版，采自《西汉南越王墓》下卷图版48，文物出版社，1991年。

［图十五:2］青铜印花凸版线图，采自《考古》1989年第2期，第178页。

4　吕烈丹:《南越王墓出土的青铜印花凸版》,《考古》1989年第2期，第178—179页；广州市文物管理委员会等:《西汉南越王墓》下卷，文物出版社，1991年，图版第48。

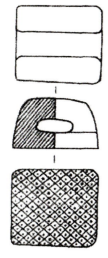

[图十六] 洛阳出土陶拍（长 14.8 厘米、宽 13 厘米），采自《文物》2004 年 7 期，第 52 页。

2]。大件花版长 5.7、宽 4.1 厘米，形状近似小树，正面是凸起的阳线构成的火焰纹，阳线与铜器底板的垂直距离约 0.1 厘米；小件花版长 3.4、最宽 1.8 厘米，形状近似"人"字形，正面有凸起的云纹，凸纹厚约 0.02 厘米。

2002 年，在洛阳东周王城内的东周至汉代的陶窑遗址中出土一件陶拍[5]，陶拍主体是一个扁平的方形拍板，拍板正面满饰小菱形纹，背面有一桥形手柄 [图十六]。

上面三件工具，材质有别，施用的对象不同，但其用途是一样的，都是印制花纹图案的印花工具，都属于印模。据此，我们推测洛阳汉砖画像印模的结构应与上面的印花工具一样，印模主体是一块扁平的木板，木板正面雕刻阳纹画像，背面有一个用于捉握的手柄。

3. 印模画像

砖上的画像和印模上的画像（简称印模画像）凹凸效果正好相反。砖上的画像是阴纹、凹面，印模画像则是阳纹、凸面。所以，根据砖上画像的情景，我们可以推知印模画像的情况。

通过对考古和博物馆藏品观察，洛阳西汉墓砖上的画像大部分是由低于砖面的阴线条构成的阴纹画像。印制这种阴纹画像的印模画像，正如西汉南越王墓出土的两块青铜印花凸版一样，印模上只有凸起的线条，线条之外是宽窄不同的凹槽或凹面。此外，洛阳汉砖上还有两种为数不多的画像类型：一种类型是画像上除了阴纹线条，还有凹面，而且凹面上有阳纹线条，如一些马画像，马头、身体和四肢是阴纹线条，马鬃、马尾则是一个窄长的凹面，凹面上有细密的凸起线条 [图十七：1—2]。故印制这种画像

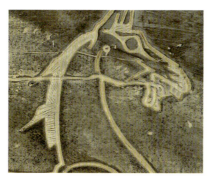

[图十七：1] 马画像马鬃

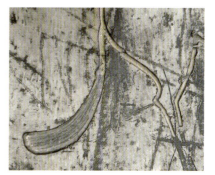

[图十七：2] 洛阳古代艺术博物馆藏砖上的马画像马尾

5 安亚伟：《东周王城战国至汉代陶窑遗址发掘简报》，《文物》2004 年 7 期，第 41—54 页。

［图十八：1］浮雕鹤画像　　　　　　　　　［图十八：2］鹤画像

的印模画像除了有凸起的线条，还有凸起的平面，而且在凸起的平面上再刻划线条。另一种类型是浅浮雕画像，这种画像数量更少，只在加拿大皇家安大略博物馆收藏的两块砖上有发现，编号 931.13.136 砖上有两个不同造型的鹤画像，鹤的轮廓线是阴纹，而身体是浮雕，身体表面还有表示羽毛的线条［图十八：1］和［图十八：2］右边的鹤。印制这种浮雕画像的印模画像的轮廓线为阳纹，轮廓线以内的底板是下凹的弧面，弧面底部再刻划线条。用这样的印模印出的画像会因工匠用力大小不同而出现不同的效果，用力大的是浮雕效果，用力小的是平面效果，［图十八：2］上的两只鹤画像是用同一个印模印制的，左边那只模印力度小，只显示出鹤的轮廓线条，鹤的身体是平面，右边的一只鹤模印力度大，直至印模底部，不仅使鹤身部分成了凸出砖面的浅浮雕，还使印模底部的羽毛线条也显示出来。

根据砖上阴纹线条的深度、宽度和底部的形状，可以推知印模上阳纹线条的大致情况，阳线高度一般为 0.1—0.2 厘米，最高达 0.4 厘米，宽度约 0.2—0.5 厘米，线条的顶部形状有平、尖、圆三种。

砖上画像是印模画像的镜像，直接反映出印模画像的雕刻水平。洛阳画像空心砖上大画幅的画像很多，就加拿大皇家安大略博物馆收藏的54块砖上的画像而言，高度（或长度）在 10—20 厘米的画像有 33 种，20—30 厘米的有 20 种，30 厘米以上的有 6 种。大幅画像为画师和雕刻工匠充分发挥和展示其高超艺术造诣和水平提供空间。由砖上那些优质画像可以看出，印模画像制作的异常细致、精美，形神兼备，生动传神地表现出各种人物、动物的外部特征和内心世界，以及人物的衣冠、武器、佩饰［图十九］。

总之，洛阳西汉空心砖画像印模是由木板制成，主体是一块扁平的、形状和大小不统一的木板，木板背面有一个把柄，正面是细致、精美的阳纹画像。

［图十九］刻画精致细腻的画像

三、"问题画像"的成因

工匠在印制画像的过程中，如果用力不匀，印出的画像会深浅不一，或出现印模边框；如果印模不是垂直角度按下，而且印模的一侧在刚刚触及砖面时出现滑动，印出的画像会产生重影或局部重影。这几种问题的出现完全是因为工匠的疏忽大意造成的。但那些存在线条断开或错位问题的画像是什么原因造成的呢？除了工匠的疏忽，应该与印模本身状况有直接关系。

洛阳西汉空心砖上明显出现线条断开或错位现象的画像有六例。其中两例是尺幅巨大的龙纹画像，其他四例是尺幅不算大的执戈武士、马、虎和长尾凤鸟画像。

我们先看尺幅巨大的龙纹画像。加拿大皇家安大略博物馆有两块龙纹画像砖，一块是长方形砖［图二十］，一块是三角形砖［图二十一］。两块砖上的画像相同，一面是武士御龙画像，另一面是青龙画像。据观察，长

[图二十] 长方形龙纹砖（砖长 119 厘米、宽 62 厘米、厚 16.5 厘米）

[图二十：1] 武士御龙画像（画像长约 88 厘米、高 36 厘米）　　　　[图二十：2] 青龙画像

[图二十一] 三角形龙纹砖（砖底长 107 厘米、高 81.5 厘米、厚 17.5 厘米）

[图二十一：1] 武士御龙画像（画像长 78 厘米、高 58.1 厘米）　　　　[图二十一：2] 青龙画像

　　方形砖上的武士御龙画像在龙角、龙腹和龙尾三个部位存在线条断开并且错位的现象 [图二十二：1]、[图二十三：1]（黄色圆圈标注的部位），龙腹、龙尾部位有少量印模边框的痕迹 [图二十三]（黄色箭头指示的部位）。龙角、龙腹两处虽不见印模边框的痕迹，但这两处断裂可用直线连接。这些迹象表明，武士御龙画像不是用刻着完整龙纹的、独立的一块印模印制的，而是将龙纹分割成四段分别刻在四块印模上。印制龙画像时将四块印模组合起来使用，第一块印模上刻龙首龙颈、第二块刻龙躯武士、第三块刻龙尾前半部、第四块刻龙尾后半部 [图二十四：1]，这四块印模的形状和大小都不一样，第二块最大，长 32.4 厘米，高 45 厘米（从龙角到龙爪）。由龙腹、龙爪、龙尾三处的印模痕迹可以看出，印模边框与画像轮廓线非常靠近，有的紧贴着画像。三角形砖上的武士御龙画像，在龙角、龙腹和龙尾三个部

[图二十二]武士
御龙画像龙角、
龙腹部位线条断
开与错位情况

[图二十二：1]长方形砖　　　　　[图二十二：2]三角形砖

[图二十三]
武士御龙画
像龙腹、龙
尾部位线条
断开与错位
情况

[图二十三：1]长方形砖　　　　　[图二十三：2]三角形砖

[图二十四]武士御龙画像四块印模示意图

[图二十四：1]长方形砖　　　　　[图二十四：2]三角形砖

［图二十五］青龙画像
龙颈、龙腹部位线条
断开与错位情况

［图二十五：1］长方形砖　　　　［图二十五：2］三角形砖

位同样存在线条断开与错位的现象［图二十二：2］、［图二十三：2］，表明它也是用四块印模印制的［图二十四：2］。另一面的青龙画像与武士御龙画像情况类似，在龙颈、颈腹、尾部也存在线条错位和印模边框痕迹的现象［图二十五］、［图二十六］，表明青龙画像也是用四块印模印制的［图二十七：1—2］。长方形砖上的青龙画像存在的问题较多，龙首重影，龙尾部的两块印模交界处的线条出现叠压现象，龙尾部位多处留下印模边框的痕迹。

　　因为砖形的差别，两块砖上的两种龙纹画像的姿态不同，长方形砖上的龙画像平直，三角形砖上的略微上仰，给人的感觉它们是用不同的印模印制的。但是，我们将两种砖上的武士御龙画像按照四块印模的分界线剪开，把相同的部位上下叠加，发现两幅画像上的线条竟十分吻合，因此可以断定，两砖上的武士御龙画像是用同一副印模制作的。两砖上的青龙画像情况一样，也是用同一副印模印出的。

　　两种龙纹画像上的线条断开和错位的位置相同，都位于两块印模的交界处。产生的原因是工匠在模印画像时没有处理好两块印模之间（或者是刚印在砖上的画像与即将印的印模之间）的衔接关系，两者没有贴紧，有时

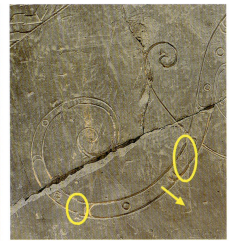

[图二十六：1]长方形砖　　　　　　[图二十六：2]三角形砖

[图二十七]
青龙画像四
块印模

[图二十七：1]长方形砖

[图二十七：2]三角形砖

上下还有微小的错位，使原本应该无缝对接的线条出现了问题，即画像线条断开和错位的问题是由于使用多块印模组合印制产生的。那么，多块印模是怎样组合的呢？是按照从首到尾的顺序一块一块分段模印的？还是像怀履光所说的，把四块印模以企口榫的连接方式连成一体，然后一次性印出整个画像[6]？通过观察画像上的各种现象和痕迹，我们认为应该是用前一种方式。

就艺术效果而言，三角形砖上的两种龙纹画像明显优于长方形砖。从姿态、气势上看，三角形砖上的龙呈上升之状，

6《中国（洛阳）古墓砖图考》，第27页。

那名武士昂头抬眼、扬盾挥剑，两脚前高后低，蓄势待发，气势强大。从模印水平看，三角形砖上画像质量要高于长方形砖，由图二十二、二十三、二十五、二十六可以看出，三角形砖上画像印模之间的衔接处理较好，线条断开错位现象明显要小。从图二十四、二十七可以看出，在三角形砖上模印画像时，印模与砖底边基本呈垂直状，易于掌握，在长方形砖上模印画像时，印模与砖底边有个不易把握的角度。此外，从存世数量看，三角形龙纹砖数量远远多于长方形砖。据我们掌握的资料，现存的三角形龙纹砖有 11 块，加拿大皇家安大略博物馆 1 块，宜阳县文物保护管理所 4 块[7]，故宫博物院 2 块[8]，美国尼尔森—阿特金斯博物馆 2 块[9]，日本东京帝国大学工业部 2 块[10]。长方形龙纹砖有确切收藏地点的目前只有 2 块，加拿大皇家安大略博物馆 1 块，美国匹兹堡卡内基艺术博物馆 1 块[11]，郭若愚的《模印砖画》书中收录一块长方形龙纹砖拓片，不知原砖现在何处[12]。因此，我们认为两幅龙纹画像是专为三角形砖设计制作的，用它印制长方形砖上的龙纹纯属"客串"。与三角形砖相比，长方形砖是长度有余而高度不足，无法按照三角形砖上的龙纹姿态和模印法式模印，工匠只能因地制宜地调整印模的角度，于是有了长方形砖上的姿态平直的龙画像。长方形砖上的青龙画像，在印模交界处两边的线条存在两个现象：第一、龙首、龙颈部分（在第一块印模上）重影，紧随其后的龙躯（在第二块印模上）没有重影［图二十五：1］；第二、龙尾前半部（在第三块印模上）后端线条与龙尾后半部（在第四块印模上）前端线条不仅错位而且还有叠压，龙尾后半部线条压在龙尾前半部的线条上［图二十六：1］。如果像怀履光所说印模是连在一块的，上述现象是不会出现的，这说明，龙画像是按照龙首→龙身→龙尾的顺序分块印制的。

收藏在其他地方的三角形龙纹砖，龙纹画像呈现的情况与加拿大皇家安大略博物馆的类似。宜阳牌窑西汉画像空心砖墓中的四块三角形龙纹砖位于墓室的前后山墙，砖的上部均被倾斜放置的墓顶砖遮挡，只露出画像砖的下部，砖上的画像一面涂红、白、黄三种颜色，另一面只涂白色。发掘简

7　洛阳地区文管会：《宜阳县牌窑西汉画像砖墓清理简报》，《中原文物》1985 年第 4 期，第 5—12 页。

8　故宫博物院：《故宫雕塑馆》，故宫出版社，2015 年，第 203—204 页。

9　沈辰提供信息。

10　［日本］下中弥三郎：《世界美术全集》，［日本］平凡社，1929 年第三卷第 83 页。

11　沈辰提供信息。

12　郭若愚：《模印砖画》，艺苑真赏社，1954 年，图版第 49—50。

[图二十八] 宜阳牌窑汉墓龙纹砖（砖底长 103 厘米、高 80 厘米）徐婵菲拍摄

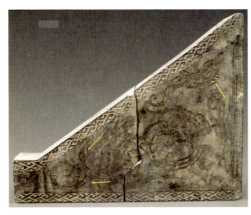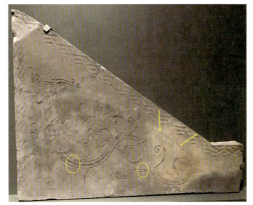

[图二十九] 故宫博物院藏（砖底长 104 厘米、高 82 厘米）　[图三十] 美国尼尔森－阿特金斯博物馆藏　沈辰拍摄
采自《故宫雕塑馆》第 203 页，故宫出版社，2015 年。

报称："……整个龙体以四块阴纹印模，在砖坯上印出龙的形象而成为阴纹平面画像。"[13] 从显露的部分我们可以看到砖上存在三处线条断开的现象［图二十八］。故宫收藏的两块三角形龙纹砖，画像模印得极好，不存在线条错位现象，但仔细观察仍可发现印模交界处两边线条的间隙。其中一块砖上的青龙画像留下两处印模的痕迹，一处在尾部，那是第二块印模右边框线，另一处在龙首上颌牙齿的下方［图二十九］。美国尼尔森—阿特金斯博物馆收藏的两块三角形龙纹砖，其中一块在武士御龙画像的龙尾部位留下印模边框痕迹，这个痕迹是第三块印模的上边框线和右上角［图三十］，藉此痕迹可知第三块印模上边框是斜直线。以上情况说明，这几块三角形龙纹砖

---

13 《宜阳县牌窑西汉画像砖墓清理简报》。"整个龙体以四块阴纹印模"中之"阴"字，当是"阳"字。

[图三十一] 执戈武士画像（高 27.3 厘米、宽 15 厘米）

[图三十一：1]　　　　　　　　　[图三十一：2]

应是一个作坊、一批工匠、一副印模制作的。

　　再看另四例尺幅不大的画像。第一例是执戈武士画像，执戈武士有两种样式，只有一种样式出现问题 [图三十一：1—2]，这是同一块砖上同一面的两个武士画像，左边的武士只有颈、肩部的线条稍有断开 [图三十一：1]，右边的武士从上到下每根线条都断开，且左高右低，错位严重 [图三十一：2]；第二例是马画像，砖上的马画像有近 20 种样式，只有两种样式出现问题，此为其中一种 [图三十二：1—2]，左边的马画像腿部线条严重错位 [图三十二：1]，右边的马画像，在马腿和马腹、马尻、马尾两处有线条断开的现象，在马腿周边和胸前有两处印模边框痕迹 [图三十二：2]；第三例是长尾凤鸟画像 [图三十三：1—2]，左边凤鸟画像中间有一条横贯身体断开 [图三十三：1]，右边凤鸟画像在断裂线的下方右侧留下了印模边框的痕迹 [图三十三：2]；第四例是虎画像，虎有 6 种样式，唯有这一种在画像上出现三条深浅不一的条带 [图三十四]。难道第四例画像和龙纹画像一样，也是将画像分段制出多块印模？第四例画像只是同种画像中诸多

[图三十二]马画像（高21厘米、宽23厘米）

[图三十二：1]　　　　　　　　　　　　　　　　　　[图三十二：2]

[图三十三]凤鸟画像（高14厘米、宽19.5厘米）：

[图三十三：1]郑州市华夏文化艺术博物馆藏砖上的凤　　[图三十三：2]
鸟画像

[图三十四]郑州市华夏文化艺术博物馆藏砖上的虎画像（高11厘米、宽19.4厘米）

［图三十五］寿星印模正面及模印画像（长 25.4 厘米、宽 16 厘米、厚 2.6 厘米）

样式中的一种，其他样式画像是由一块印模印制，为什么单单这一例要分制多模呢？这不合情理。福建省泉州市博物馆收藏的民国时期印制版画的木质阳纹印模实物，为我们解答这个疑问提供了有益的线索。

泉州博物馆收藏有 9 件印模，楠木制成，皆为长方形，长 23.1—27 厘米，宽 16—19.9 厘米，厚 2.2—3.8 厘米。7 件是双面阳刻，2 件是单面阳刻[14]。我们来看其中的两件：一件是寿星印模，用一整块木板雕成，双面阳刻，正面刻寿星画像［图三十五］，背面刻仙女画像。这件印模为我们展现了阳纹印模的模样，旁边印出的画像，形象地反映出印模画像与印模印出的画像之间左右镜像的关系。另一件是福禄寿三星印模，双面阳刻，正面刻福禄寿三星画像［图三十六：1］，背面刻一男（左）一女（右）两位侍者画像［图三十六：2］，两面画像周边有阳纹边框。印模正面上方横贯三星的头部有一条比较细且稍有弯曲的裂缝，下方横贯三星脚踝处有一条宽而直的裂缝，背面男侍画像上有一条宽而直的纵向裂缝，女侍画像的上方有条很短的裂缝，旁边印出的画像清楚的反映出印模上的裂缝情况。如果只看印模印出的图片，我们会认为印模是断开的，或者是画像刻在两块木板上。通过与文章作者沟通后得知，9 件印模都用单独一块木板雕成，印模上阳纹线条的高度都是 0.2 厘米，福禄寿三星印模的两面各有两条程度不同的裂

14　盛荣红：《馆藏精品民国木印模赏析》，《文物鉴定与鉴赏》2017 年第 3 期，第 13—21 页。

[图三十六]福禄寿三星印模正背面及模印画像（长23.4厘米、宽19.9厘米、厚2.2厘米）

[图三十六：1]正面

[图三十六：2]背面

缝，但印模没有断开。

　　据此，我们认为，执戈武士等四种画像的印模也是由一整块木板制作而成，因为使用时间久了，印模出现了裂缝。使用有裂缝的印模印出的画像，线条自然是断开的。至于武士和马画像上的线条错位现象，我们推测，可能是印模出现了更大的问题——断成两块，工匠对印模简单修整一下坚持用它印完这批砖上的画像。这一点从每个执戈武士画像线条错位程度不同可以得到证实。因为画像是一次印出，印完后即使出错也难以修改，只能任其留在砖上。

四、结语

通过对洛阳西汉阴纹画像空心砖上问题画像的观察与分析，我们对印制阴纹画像的阳纹印模有了更进一步的认识。阳纹印模的特征主要有：第一，印模用木材制成，印模背面应该有把柄，正面雕刻阳纹画像；第二，印模的形状多种多样，有的或有边框，有的没有边框，而是随着画像的轮廓变化而变化；第三，大多数的印模上面只雕一个画像，即一模一像，少数印模上面雕2—4个画像，如大雁、鹤等，唯有尺幅巨大的龙纹画像印模例外，是多模一像；第四，印模画像制作精美，艺术水平极高。

洛阳阴纹画像以其画幅大，精致美观，艺术水平高超著称于世，但它流行时间短，流传地域有限，砖的数量不多（远远少于阳纹画像砖），其主要原因是印制阴纹画像的阳纹印模制作难度大，费时耗力又容易磨损、毁坏，限制了画像砖的生产数量，难以满足社会化大批量生产的需求。所以，它很快就被形状规整（多为长方形）、尺幅不大、制作容易的阳纹画像取代了。

如今，阴纹画像空心砖虽在，其制作技艺（包括空心砖的制作）已难以说清道明。洛阳阴纹画像砖艺术仿佛一颗在遥远的夜空中闪烁着神秘光芒的星辰，引发人们无限的遐思与猜想。

原载《故宫博物院院刊》2020年第2期

洛阳西汉画像空心砖的发现与研究

徐婵菲　［加拿大］沈　辰

一、概述

　　1939 年，怀履光编著的《中国古墓砖图考》由加拿大多伦多大学出版。此书以 20 世纪 30 年代前后出土于洛阳金村一带的 55 块阴纹画像空心砖为研究对象，从砖的出土地点、铭文、年代、制作和画像内容等诸多方面进行了考证，并根据墓砖的形状和砖上的文字对画像砖墓做了复原研究。这在当时缺乏科学发掘材料和相关研究资料的背景条件下，对于一个对中国文化了解有限的外国人，实属难能可贵。书中的内容、观点、研究视角和方法，就是在今天看来仍有巨大的参考、借鉴价值。

　　20 世纪二三十年代的中国，军阀割据，国弱民贫。洛阳百姓为谋生计，掘墓盗宝，致使许多古墓惨遭毁坏。遭盗掘的诸多古墓当中，有一种用大型空心砖砌建的古墓，因为墓砖形制特别，而且不少砖上装饰有精致的画像，遂引起古董商人和外籍人士关注，争相购买，甚至预先付钱，坐等出土，致使画像空心砖价格倍增，盗掘活动更加猖獗[1]。因为是盗掘而出，墓葬的形制、结构和墓砖的位置都难以确知。从《中国古墓砖图考》一书和怀履光

1　丁士选：《圹砖琐言》：“甚且预付现款，坐待掘物，致砖价倍徙，盗风渐炽。”北平燕京大学：《考古学社社刊》第六期，1937 年。

与加拿大皇家安大略博物馆的往来信件中，确知怀履光没有到过掘墓现场，也没有看到过任何一座画像空心砖墓。书中的两张画像空心砖墓的结构图，是他根据比利时人 F. 毕肯斯（F.Bückens）在郑州荥泽发掘的汉代空心砖墓的结构图，加上他的推测绘出来的。在研究过程中，怀氏对这批盗掘出土、丧失许多信息的墓砖资料，深感遗憾，并期待着没被盗扰的新资料。

如今，这批墓砖已出土 80 余年了。80 年间，中国社会发生了巨大的变化，中国的考古事业蓬勃开展。正如怀履光在书中所言："一定还有许多同类的其它墓葬还保存在原地，而且将来的调查会弄清楚与墓砖及其画像有关的目前尚不明白或未知的许多疑点。"据笔者统计，自 20 世纪 50 年代以来，洛阳经过科学发掘，且公布发掘报告的西汉空心砖墓已有 70 余座，为我们研究画像空心砖提供了可资参照的材料。

在此，我们试图利用现代考古材料，对本书中的画像空心砖及其相关问题做一探讨。

二、洛阳西汉画像空心砖的发现与研究

在探讨之前，我们先梳理一下有关洛阳汉代空心砖的出土历史和相关的研究。

（一）20 世纪 50 年代之前

有关汉代空心砖的记录，最早见于明代的文献。明代的曹昭在《格古要论》中提到的郭公砖就是空心砖[2]。明代的王佐和王士性在他们的著作中对郭公砖的形制、用途都作了简要的阐述[3]。说明汉代空心砖在明代就有出土。明代文献的真实性已被考古材料所证实，在洛阳发掘的明代墓葬中，就发现有汉代空心砖[4]。汉代画像空心砖的大量出土，始于 20 世纪初。1904 年 6

2 《格古要论卷之中·古琴论·琴桌》中有："琴桌须用维摩样，高二尺八寸，可入膝于桌下，阔可容三琴，长过琴一尺许。桌面郭公砖最佳，玛瑙石、南阳石、永石者尤好。"
3 （明）王佐在《新增格古要论卷一·琴桌》条目记载："……桌面用郭公砖最佳……佐尝见郭公砖，灰白色，中空，面上有象眼花纹。"（明）王士性的《广志绎》卷三中有："洛阳水土深厚，葬者至四五丈而不及泉……郭公砖长数尺，空其中，亦以甃家壁，能使千载不还于土。俗传其女能之，遂杀女以秘其法。今吴、越称以琴砖，宝之，而洛阳巨细家墙趾无不有之也。"
4 洛阳市第二文物工作队：《洛阳道北二路明墓发掘简报》，《文物》2011 年第 6 期。

月开工修筑开封至洛阳的汴洛铁路，当铁路修至洛阳邙山一带（今洛阳市区
与偃师市、孟津县交界处）时，许多古墓被推出，出土了大量的各类文物。
这些文物引起中国学者、古董商和外国人士的注意，进而大事搜索，争相
收购。盗掘古墓活动一直持续到 20 世纪 40 年代末，在这期间被破坏的古墓
难以计数，现在所说的洛阳古墓"十墓九空"的状况，即是这场旷日持久的
盗墓活动所造成的悲惨恶果。被盗掘出土和流失的珍贵文物，除了广为世人
所知两周青铜器、汉魏石经、佛教造像、墓志陶俑外，画像空心砖也是其
中重要的一类。据说，洛阳的画像空心砖"是 1925 年到 1932 年间陆续从洛
阳市东十二里地的金村被挖出来，出土的数量，据说有二三百枚，可惜大
部精粹被送到国外去了"[5]。只有一少部分留存国内[6]。有关画像空心砖的著录、
研究集中出现在 20 世纪 30 年代前后。

国内有关洛阳汉代画像砖的著录和研究主要有：

1932 年，燕京大学国学研究所编辑出版的第十一期《燕京学报》[7]的封
面上刊载一张空心砖上画像的拓本，原砖出土于洛阳金村一座汉墓。载于
封二的介绍文字为："封面乃本所所藏汉砖拓片，砖上有朱书，东北下三字，
洛阳金村出土。"

1933 年，郑德坤、沈维钧编著的《中国明器》，记录了燕京大学国学研
究所收藏的一对上面有人物画像的空心砖[8]。

1935 年，王振铎编印的《汉代圹砖集录》收录了出土于河南各处的画
像空心砖拓本，其中有洛阳出土的两块[9]。在书后的附言部分，王振铎从圹
砖的命名、制造、应用、范模分析、（画像）主要内容、（空心砖墓）营造
等几方面做了精深的研究。

1937 年，有丁士选的《圹砖琐言》[10]和许敬参的《汉朱书圹砖小记》[11]两

5　郭若愚：《模印砖画》，艺苑真赏社，1953 年出版，1956 年修订。这批砖中被运到国外的部分，
分别收藏在法国巴黎博物馆、加拿大皇家安大略博物馆、美国波士顿美术馆、美国尼尔森—阿特
金斯博物馆、日本东京帝国大学工学部，以及私人收藏家手中。
6　收藏在故宫博物院、河南博物院、北京大学、燕京大学、北京图书馆等处。
7　《燕京学报》是原燕京大学创办的学术刊物之一，旨在研究和传播中国传统文化，1927 年创刊，
1951 年因燕京大学与北京大学合并而停刊。
8　"圹砖亦可谓为明器之一。而前人亦鲜有论及者，此物之用，为筑圹及隧道所必须。本所所藏
有圹砖一对，一已中断。砖形颇大，内部透空，外印有种种图案—正面为几何式的花纹，上为孝
子像，沿边多长方小窟；侧面孝子像，沿边亦多长方小窟。"郑德坤、沈维钧：《中国明器》，上海
文艺出版社据哈佛燕京社 1933 年 1 月版影印，1992 年。
9　王振铎：《汉代圹砖集录》，北平考古学社印石印本二百部，1935 年，图八、图九。
10　丁士选：《圹砖琐言》，北平燕京大学《考古学社社刊》第六期，1937 年。
11　许敬参：《汉朱书圹砖小记》，《河南博物馆馆刊》第十一集，1937 年。

篇研究性的文章。《圹砖琐言》对空心砖的名称、制作、形制、纹饰和空心砖墓的形制做了研究和推测。《汉朱书圹砖小记》对收藏于河南博物院的 11 块有朱书文字的画像空心砖的形制和砖上的文字进行了详细的介绍，并对砖的排列使用做了初步的推测。

1939 年，时为河南大学校长的王广庆，将其在 1932—1933 年间访察洛阳古墓、碑刻时的见闻，写成《洛阳访古记》一文。文中有一段关于洛阳画像空心砖的文字，内容涉及空心砖古今称谓、尺寸大小、砖上的画像和文字、出土历史背景、价格和流失国外等诸多方面[12]。虽然简要，但内容丰富，信息量大，是研究早期出土的洛阳画像空心砖的珍贵资料。

国外的记载和研究主要有：

1904—1908 年修筑陇海铁路（开封至洛阳段）时，对古物有浓厚兴趣和知识的比利时人 F. 毕肯斯因为是铁路局总医官，在修路过程中，他在郑州的荥泽和洛阳调查了见到的空心砖墓。后来将墓葬资料发表在 1921 年第 46 期《布鲁塞尔人类学协会通讯》（法文版）上。文中详细描述了他见到的空心砖墓，并把空心砖墓分为四型，墓顶的形状有平顶和屋形顶，并附有平顶型空心砖墓的照片[13]。

1923 年，日本美术史学家大村西崖编辑的《获古图录》中收录有两块洛阳出土的画像空心砖的拓本。关于这两块画像空心砖，书中有一段说明："此种大砖，未见前人著录，它们是近些年刚出土的，但数量很多，流传到日本的为数不少。砖上花纹大概是用木模压印出来的。它们多数为壁砖，其中也有柱砖。从柱砖的大小来看，可推测这些柱砖多数是用于建造墓室的。有些壁砖也可能是用于建造地面上的祠堂。这里登载的两块砖，一块上面有手持武器的人物与马匹的画像，另一块上有树木和马匹的画像，上面还盖有凤鸟的画像。很多画像是重复出现的。据此，很容易看出它们是同一印模印制的。砖上人物、马匹的画法很独特。把它们和东汉画像石相比较，

---

12 王广庆：《洛阳访古记》，《河南文史资料》第 23 辑，1987年。"所谓郭公砖者，今亦名琴砖，乡人则名为通古砖，厚可四、五寸，广尺二四寸不等，中空，一端无横当，一端横当上有圆孔，四面小型图案画，历历成行列，亦有奔马、神鸟等图画，意态生动，非寻常工人所为。殆作坯时，刻名家手迹，压印而成。其上往往存朱书'上二、西五、中三'等字迹，必为整圹壁时记注位次之符，其亦黄肠题凑之遗制软？洛阳附近各县，修路筑墓，往往于地下得之。精品一方，亦可直银币一二版。城乡民户，多用作庭园中花盆基台，亦有辇载出境者"。

13 详见 O. 喜龙仁（O.Siren）的《早期中国艺术史》第二卷（《History of Early Chinese Art, Volume II》）。

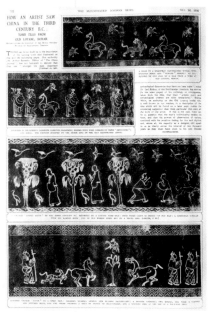

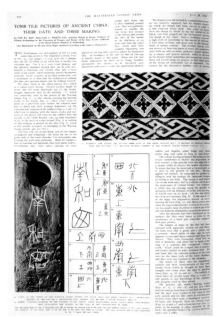

［图1］《伦敦新闻画报》

可知这种砖可能为汉晋之物。"

1926年，大村西崖在他的《中国美术史》一书中也提到了汉代画像空心砖[14]。

1929年，下中弥三郎在《世界美术全集（3）》中收录了两块三角形龙纹画像砖[15]。

1930年，德国人奥托·费舍尔（Otto Fischer）在他的《中国汉代绘画》[16]书中收录了几块画像空心砖，其中一块是三角形龙纹空心砖。据王振铎所言，关野贞的《支那工艺图鉴·瓦砖篇》[17]解说册中谈到空心砖，除用于建造地下墓室外，还用于建造地上的墓阙、祠堂，书中还绘有平顶形空心砖墓的结构图和斜坡顶形空心砖墓的墓门正面图[18]。

1935年，在伦敦举办的中国艺术展览会，展览会上展出了汉代画像空心砖的拓片，这些拓片颇受人关注。后来，《伦敦新闻画报》（the Illustrated London News，1936年10月24日和1937年7月24日）刊载了比较详细的介绍［图1］。

1939年，怀履光出版专著《中国古墓砖图考》。

（二）20世纪50年代之后

20世纪50年代中华人民共和国成立后，盗掘古墓、走私文物活动得到有效的遏制。洛阳市配合城市基本建设进行的考古勘探、发掘和文物普查工作持续开展，并取得了丰硕的成果，画像空心砖的资料也有很大的

14　［日本］大村西崖著，陈彬龢译：《中国美术史》，商务印书馆，1926年，第25页。

15　［日本］下中弥三郎：《世界美术全集（3）》，平凡社，1929年，图122。砖上的画像与加拿大皇家安大略博物馆和宜阳牌窑空心砖墓的三角形龙纹砖一样，一面是武士持盾御龙，另一面是龙纹，但砖上没有涂彩。

16　［德国］奥托·费舍尔：《中国汉代绘画》，1930年。

17　［日本］关野贞：《支那工艺图鉴·瓦砖篇》，日本帝国工艺会，1932年。

18　王振铎：《汉代炉砖集录》，北平考古学社，1935年。

收获。这一时期，画像空心砖有两个来源，一是考古发掘，二是从民间征集。考古发掘出土的画像空心砖数量不多。据统计，1949 年以来洛阳经过科学发掘且已公布发掘报告的西汉空心砖墓有 72 座[19]，其中只有 3 座墓出土画像砖，数量不足 30 块。另一项有关画像空心砖的重要考古发现是 1998 年出自函谷关仓库建筑遗址的一块有纪年的画像空心砖残片，砖上除了有模印的树纹和五铢钱纹外，还有一排"永始二年造"（前 15 年）的模印文字[20]。

大量的画像空心砖不是通过科学发掘获取的，而是从民间征集的。据不完全统计，自 20 世纪 50 年代以来，洛阳地区先后发现的西汉画像空心砖有将近 600 块。其中数量较多的发现主要有：

1. 1977 年，洛阳博物馆对邙山一带的西汉画像砖进行了一次系统的调查和征集，共收集 500 多块画像空心砖[21]。砖上的画像绝大部分是阴纹，只有极少数为阳纹。这批画像砖的基本情况，见黄明兰著的《洛阳汉代画像砖》。

2. 1984 年 5—11 月，洛阳市文物工作队在洛阳市郊及所属的孟津、偃师、新安三县进行文物普查，发现 20 余块西汉画像空心砖[22]。砖上画像都是阴纹。画像种类和内容与本书和《洛阳汉代画像砖》相同。

3. 1985 年前后，河南博物院在洛阳邙山一带调查征集到一批西汉画像空心砖，数量不详[23]。

4. 1984 —1991 年，洛阳市第二文物工作队在伊川、宜阳、洛宁、孟津县等地发现一批西汉画像空心砖[24]。报告未说明画像砖的具体数量，根据文中的介绍，至少有 17 块砖。画像以阳纹为主。

这一时期有关洛阳西汉画像空心砖的研究著作与图录主要有：

1954 年出版的郭若愚的《模印砖画》[25]。此书以图片为主，前后附有少量介绍画像砖的出土背景、形制和画像内容的文字。书中的画像砖都是 20 世纪 50 年代之前出土的，其中前 43 页的画像砖拓本与本书中的拓本相同，

19　这里统计的空心砖墓，是指用空心砖，或以空心砖为主建造的墓葬。据笔者了解，洛阳发掘的空心砖墓数量很多，但许多材料没有公布。

20　洛阳市第二文物工作队：《黄河小浪底盐东村汉函谷关仓库建筑遗址发掘简报》，《文物》2000 年 10 期。

21　洛阳市文物工作队：《历程——洛阳市文物工作队三十年》，文物出版社，2011 年，第 236 页。

22　张湘：《洛阳新发现的西汉空心画像砖》，《文物》1990 年第 2 期。

23　周到、王景荃：《河南文化大典·文物典·画像砖》，中州古籍出版社，2008 年。

24　李献奇、杨海钦：《洛阳又发现一批西汉空心画像砖》，《文物》1993 年第 5 期。

25　郭若愚：《模印砖画》，艺苑真赏社，1953 年出版，1956 年修订。

应是拓自同一块砖。

1959 年出版的《洛阳烧沟汉墓》[26]。《洛阳烧沟汉墓》中有 28 座空心砖墓的资料，但没有画像砖墓。书中总结了空心砖墓的发展演变序列，同时对空心砖的形制、制作和花纹进行了考查研究。这对我们研究画像空心砖有极大的参考价值。

1986 年出版的黄明兰编著的《洛阳汉画像砖》[27]。此书图文并茂，是目前仅见的一部全面介绍洛阳画像空心砖的著作。在书的前面有一篇《洛阳汉画像砖概述》，从画像空心砖的兴起、制造、出土地点和范围、分类、时代、艺术特点，画像砖上的花纹、文字，画像空心砖墓的形制等诸多方面做了阐述，特别是空心砖的制作部分，尤为详细。

2001 年出版的蒋英炬、杨爱国编著的《汉代画像石与画像砖》[28]。

2008 年出版的周到、王景荃编著的《河南文化大典·文物典·画像砖》[29]。

研究文章数量很多，不一一列举。

这一时期国外的研究及著录主要有：

1974 年，大阪市立美术馆举办展览，展览中有两块洛阳出土的汉代画像空心砖[30]。

1986 年，土居淑子编著的《古代中国的画像石》书中，收录两块洛阳出土的汉代画像空心砖[31]。

三、以考古材料研究散存的西汉画像空心砖

由上文可知，洛阳的画像空心砖绝大部分不是出自考古发掘。因此，与画像空心砖有关的许多问题，譬如，画像砖的时代、画像砖所属的墓葬的形制、画像砖在墓中的方位等，都很难说清楚了。

要解决上述问题，只有依靠现代考古材料。目前，洛阳经过科学发掘

26　洛阳区考古发掘队：《洛阳烧沟汉墓》，科学出版社，1959 年，第 84—91 页。
27　黄明兰：《洛阳汉画像砖》，河南美术出版社，1986 年。
28　蒋英炬、杨爱国：《汉代画像石与画像砖》，文物出版社，2001 年。
29　周到、王景荃：《河南文化大典·文物典·画像砖》，中州古籍出版社，2008 年。
30　［日本］大阪市立美术馆：《汉代的美术》，1974 年，第 44 页，图 5—7，第 45 页，图 5—6。
31　［日本］土居淑子：《古代中国的画像石》，［日本］日本株式会社同朋社，1986 年。

并出土有画像空心砖的墓只有三座，它们是 1985 年发掘的宜阳县牌窑西汉画像砖墓 [32]、1990 年发掘的偃师县新莽壁画墓 [33] 和 1992 年发掘的洛阳浅井头西汉空心砖壁画墓 [34]。这三座墓不仅是我们研究洛阳画像空心砖墓形制和时代的基础性材料，也是我们重新认识那些早年被盗掘出土、丧失了许多原始信息的散存于世界各地的画像空心砖的极为宝贵的参照资料。

本书中的画像空心砖，皆为阴纹画像砖，1930 年前后出于洛阳金村，后由加拿大传教士怀履光收购，于 1931 年入藏加拿大皇家安大略博物馆。核查该馆的藏品入藏登记表，这批砖只有 55 块，其中三角形砖 8 块、长方形砖 47 块。为叙述方便，我们将这批砖称为"怀氏砖"。洛阳科学发掘的三座画像空心砖墓，只有宜阳县牌窑西汉画像砖墓中的画像砖，与"怀氏砖"在砖的形制和砖上画像的内容、艺术风格等方面比较一致，故而依据宜阳画像砖墓的材料来探讨"怀氏砖"。

（一）宜阳县牌窑西汉画像砖墓概况

宜阳县牌窑西汉画像砖墓，由墓道、甬道、墓室组成。甬道、墓室用空心砖砌成。墓室为长方形，墓顶是斜坡形顶，南北长 3.8、东西宽 1.7、高 2.25 米。墓室的砌法是：底部平铺一层空心砖；南壁开设墓门，墓门由门框、门楣、门槛四块空心砖组成，门扉为木质，已腐朽不存。门楣之上用 2 块直角三角形砖组成山墙；东、西两壁各用四块空心砖，分两层侧立错缝叠砌。8 块壁砖上有 6 块砖上刻有文字，文字是"西北上""西北下""东北上""东北下""东南上""东南下。"壁砖之上再平铺一层空心砖；北壁用 2 块长方形空心砖侧立叠砌。这两块砖朝向墓室一面的砖面两端有长 0.22、厚 0.15 米榫头。两层壁砖之上用两块三角形砖组成山墙；墓顶用特制的两端抹去一角的柱形空心砖砌成斜坡形顶［图 2］[35]。

全墓用 89 块空心砖砌成。甬道用砖 12 块，皆为几何纹砖。墓室用砖

32 洛阳地区文管会：《宜阳县牌窑西汉画像砖墓清理简报》，《中原文物》1985 年 4 期。
33 洛阳市第二文物工作队：《洛阳偃师县新莽壁画墓清理简报》，《文物》1992 年 12 期。墓中有彩绘壁画，有 4 块阳纹画像空心砖。
34 洛阳市第二文物工作队：《洛阳浅井头西汉壁画墓发掘简报》，《文物》1993 年 5 期。墓中有彩绘壁画，有 6 块画像空心砖。
35 此墓发掘后被搬迁复原到宜阳县灵山寺西边山腰上。2012 年 11 月、2014 年 5 月笔者两次去复原的墓葬中考察。此图为笔者根据发掘简报中的墓葬平剖面图结合实地考察后重新绘制，本文中的照片也是在现场考察时拍摄的。

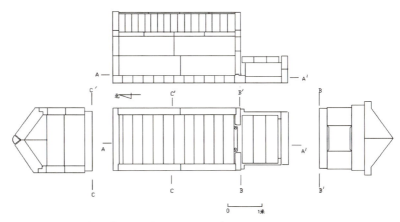

［图 2］宜阳县牌窑西汉画像砖墓平、剖面图

77 块，其中有 15 块是画像砖。画像砖的两面都有画像，有一面画像上涂彩。前壁、左壁、右壁的墓砖涂彩的一面朝向墓室，后壁的墓砖涂彩的一面朝向墓室外［图 3—4］。

15 块画像砖中有三角形砖 4 块，砖的形制、尺寸、画像都一样［图 5］。砖的底长 1.08 米、高 0.8 米、厚 0.18 米。砖的一面是一条龙，另一面是武士御龙，边纹都是菱形纹。4 块砖两两组合位于前后山墙部位，朝向墓室的

［图 3］墓室后壁（从南向北拍摄）

［图 4］墓室前壁及墓门（从北向南拍摄）

［图 5］三角形武士持盾御龙砖

［图 6］前壁山墙龙纹砖局部

［图 7］前壁山墙武士御龙砖局部

砖面上部被墓顶砖遮挡，所以砖面上的龙纹只露出下半部［图 6—7］。

长方形砖 11 块，砖的尺寸大小差别不大，砖长 1.79—1.82 米、宽 0.41—0.55 米、厚 0.18—0.19 米。分别位于左、右、后三壁和门楣部位。两块后壁砖与其他砖略有差别，在面朝墓室的砖面的两端被削去 0.03 米厚的一片，做出长 0.22 米的榫头。榫头的作用是卡住与之相邻的、成直角转折的左右壁砖，避免其向墓内倾倒。长方形砖上模印马、树、虎、凤鸟画像，有的画像上涂彩，有的砖上彩绘出玉璧和山峦［图 8—15］。各砖上的画像组合见表一。

宜阳画像砖墓出土有随葬器物，根据墓形和器物判断此墓年代为西汉中期。

[图 8]"东北上"砖涂彩画像

[图 9]"西北上"砖涂彩画像和彩绘山峦

[图 10]"东南上"砖涂彩画像和刻画文字

[图 11]门楣砖上涂彩画像

[图 12]涂彩画像

[图 13]虎

[图 14]彩绘玉璧

［图 15］彩绘玉璧

表一　宜阳墓长方形画像砖画像组合

		东壁		后（北）壁	西壁		南壁门楣砖
上层	砖上文字	东南上	东北上		西北上		
	砖上画像	朝向墓室一面：虎、树、马、马、树、虎	朝向墓室一面：虎、树、马、树、虎	朝向墓室一面：虎、树、马、树、虎	朝向墓室一面：虎、树、马、（彩绘山峦）虎、虎	朝向墓室一面：虎、树、马、马、树、虎	
		另一面：马、树、虎，组合不明	另一面：马、树、虎，组合不明	另一面：马、树、虎，组合不明	另一面：马、树、虎，组合不明	另一面：马、树、虎，组合不明	朝向墓室的一面，一字排开的3只凤鸟
下层	砖上文字	东南下	东北下		西北下		朝向墓外的一面，是7对双飞雁
	砖上画像	朝向墓室一面：虎、树、马、树、虎	朝向墓室一面：虎、树、马、树、虎	朝向墓室一面：虎、树、马、马、树、虎、双飞雁	朝向墓室一面：虎、树、马、树、虎	朝向墓室一面：虎、树、马、马、树、虎	
		另一面：马、树、虎，组合不明	另一面：马、树、虎，组合不明	另一面：马、树、虎，组合不明	另一面：马、树、虎，组合不明	另一面：马、树、虎，组合不明	

（二）怀氏砖与宜阳砖比较

宜阳墓中虽然只有 15 块画像砖，但画像砖上出现的现象比较多，包含的信息丰富。比如砖上有文字，有彩绘，有榫，最重要的是宜阳砖经过科学发掘，墓葬的结构完整，相对年代清楚，墓砖的位置、朝向明确。"怀氏砖"中有的类型、现象，在宜阳画像砖中都能找到，两批材料具有很强的可比性。

1. 砖形比较

宜阳墓中的画像砖有两种砖型，长方形砖和三角形砖，怀氏砖也只有这两种砖型。

宜阳墓的后壁砖是一种特制的两头有榫的长方形砖。怀氏砖中有一块与之形制极其相似的砖，此砖的一面的两端也被削去 1 英寸（约 2.53 厘米）厚的一片，榫长 6 英寸（约 15.24 厘米）。参照宜阳墓砖的材料，可以断定这块砖的位置在墓室的后壁，而不是像怀氏推测的位于墓室前部墓门的底部。此外，"怀氏砖"中还有一块一端有榫的砖，可以断定这块砖是壁砖，其位置或在左壁的前部，或在右壁的后部。

"怀氏砖"中有 8 块三角形砖，其中一块龙纹三角形砖与宜阳的三角形砖完全一样。由宜阳墓的材料，可断定怀氏三角形砖的位置是前后山墙部位。

2. 文字比较

宜阳砖和"怀氏砖"都有部分砖上有文字，而且文字的性质和内容是一样的。

宜阳墓有 7 块画像砖上带有指示方位的文字，其中长方形砖 6 块，三角形砖一块。

长方形砖上的文字是在砖烧好后刻上的，刻字的一面朝向墓室［图 16］。文字是三字一组，

［图 16］宜阳砖上的刻画文字"东北上"

先记方向，再记上下，单行竖读，如"西北上""西北下""东北上""东北下"等。字不大，刻得很轻，刻字时有意识地避开画像。刻字的6块砖都位于墓室的左、右两壁，实际放置位置与砖上文字指示的方位完全相符。

"怀氏砖"中有15块长方形砖上写有文字［图17］。文字的内容基本与宜阳砖一样，有"西北上""西北下""东北上""东北下""东南上""东南下""西南上""西南下""和东上""和东下"，但排列方式不同，多数是双行排列，还有横行的，有顺读的，有逆读的。参照宜阳墓砖的材料，可以断定这15块砖的位置是在墓室的左右两壁。

［图17］怀氏砖上的朱书文字"西北上"

宜阳墓中有一块三角形砖，在朝向墓室的砖面右下角有朱笔书写的"北西"二字［图18］。但这块砖没有按文字指示的方位放在西北位置，而是被放在了东南，即按文字所示这块应该在墓室后壁的右上方（山墙右侧）的砖放在了墓室前壁的左上方（山墙左侧）。这块只在一面涂彩的砖，放在现在这个位置（墓室前壁），其带彩的一面朝向墓室。如果被放在文字指示的位置（墓室后壁），其带彩的一面同样也朝向墓室，而不是现在看到的后壁山墙砖带彩一面朝向墓外的状况了。从这一现象，我们可以得到两个结论：一是砖上的颜色是在建墓之前就涂上了，二是本书第四章怀履光有关砖上文字是为了确保有彩的一面朝向墓室的看法不是完全正确的。另外，这一现象还说明，在当时可能存在这样的理念：墓室内的前壁和两壁要有颜色，后壁的外侧要有颜色。正如在许多早期的画像石墓中看到的，石板上有画像的一面往往不是朝向墓室，而是朝向墓外。

"怀氏砖"中也有一块一面带彩的三角形龙纹砖，在砖的端面上刻有"南和西"三字［图19］。怀履光对这三个字的解释是："'西'指的是山墙的西半部，'和'无疑涉及一对可组合的三角形砖，并指示它们应在墓

［图18］宜阳砖上的朱书文字"北西"

[图19] 怀氏砖上的刻
画文字 "南和西"

葬的南边入口处上方拼合在一起形成山墙。"这一解释非
常正确。此砖的位置无疑是位于墓室的山墙部位。

3. 画像比较

宜阳砖上的单体画像种类有马、树、虎、凤鸟、大
雁、龙、武士御龙等七种。这七种单体画像，在怀氏砖中
都发现，而且他们是出自同一个印模。不仅如此，有的画
像的排布、组合也完全一样，如：两匹相向而对的马。这
一现象说明，至少那些印有与宜阳砖上相同单体画像的
砖，和宜阳画像砖是来自同一个制砖作坊。

怀履光根据砖上的文字推测这些墓砖至少来自3座或
更多的墓。如上文提到的，出自金村的画像砖有二三百块，
怀氏只收购了55块（后经考证，实际为54块）。我们知
道，过去人们掘墓，是几人合作，若获得贵重古物，就等
古物卖掉后再分钱，若是普通古物如墓砖、陶器之类的，
则随时就地均分，所以很难将出自一座墓中的墓砖陶器收
集全。[36] 由现代考古发掘可知，由于长期重压，一定有不
少画像砖破碎严重，被丢弃掉。因此，怀履光推测是完全
正确的，50多块墓砖肯定来自多座墓葬。宜阳15块画像
砖的心纹是由七种单体画像相互组合、反复模印而成。长
方形画像砖上的单体画像只有五种，其中马、树、虎出现
次数最多。砖上的边纹都一样，上部边纹为勾连云纹，下
部为菱形纹。这似乎说明，同一座墓中的画像砖，砖上模
印的单体画像的种类有限，是以有限的几种单体画像，反复模印而成。同
时，砖的边纹也一样。砖的规格相似，尤其是左右两壁壁砖的高度要一样。
据此，我们就可以根据画像砖上的某几种单体画像、边纹和砖的高度，大
致把怀氏砖分组了，不同的组或许就是出自不同的墓葬。

36　丁士选：《圹砖琐言》，北平燕京大学《考古学社社刊》第六期，1937年。"如获贵重古物，
多俟售脱之后，始分物价，至于普通获物，如圹砖陶器之属，则就地随时拆散，约略匀分，故圹
砖及衬葬陶器之不易收集全份，即此故也。"

四、讨论与结论

（一）阴纹画像空心砖墓的形制

自从 20 世纪初画像空心砖被发现后，画像空心砖墓的形制、结构问题就引起人们的注意。当时正式发掘并公布材料的空心砖墓只有零星的几座[37]，而且这几座墓又不是画像空心砖墓。虽然如此，人们不免就根据这几座墓的资料对画像空心砖墓的形制进行套用、揣测。今天看来，这种做法应该是合理的，特殊性包含于普遍性之中，作为空心砖墓的一个特别类型，画像空心砖墓的形制当然不会脱离于空心砖墓的墓形之外。同理，下面我们依据洛阳的考古材料，对画像空心砖墓的形制作一探讨。

洛阳科学发掘的 72 座空心砖墓中，西汉早期墓 11 座，中期墓 48 座，晚期墓 13 座[38]，各期墓葬形制的特征如下。西汉早期空心砖墓为长方形单棺墓，墓顶以平顶为主，斜坡屋脊形顶墓只有 1 座。多数墓中出现了墓门设施（有门柱、门扉等）。所用的空心砖砖形有长方形、柱形、三角形三种，砖上的花纹只有几何纹。西汉中期空心砖墓的墓型和砖型与早期差别不大，仍以平顶墓为主，斜坡屋脊形顶墓仍为少数（只有一座），个别空心砖墓出现小砖券的弧形顶。双棺室墓数量增加，双棺室之间有空心砖砌的隔墙。砖形有长方形、柱形、三角形 3 种，画像砖出现了，画像的表现技法为阴纹，并出现在画像上涂彩的现象。西汉晚期空心砖墓规模增大，结构复杂，墓室一般为双棺室，无隔墙，墓顶以平脊斜坡式顶为主，也有小砖券弧形顶。砖形的种类增多，亚腰形砖、直角梯形砖、特型砖都在这一期出现。砖上画像的表现技法是阳纹和浅浮雕，阴纹画像消失。画像砖的数量减少，彩绘壁画出现[39]。

由考古材料可知，洛阳的画像空心砖墓分两种，阴纹画像空心砖墓和阳纹画像空心砖墓。从时间上看，阴纹画像空心砖墓出现于西汉中期，西

37　比利时人 F. 毕肯斯（F.Bückens）在郑州荥泽发掘一座空心砖墓，资料发表在 1921 年第 46 期《布鲁塞尔人类学协会通讯》上，后被 O. 喜龙仁（O.Siren）引用在他的《早期中国艺术史》第二卷书中。这一资料梅原末治也予以关注，写有《河南郑州及荥泽县发现之汉代坟墓及其遗物》一文，发表在《东洋学报》第十九卷第一号。关野贞在《支那工艺图鉴·瓦砖篇》中对空心砖墓的形制做了研究，将空心砖墓分为"纵圹式"和"横圹式"两种，并绘有数张空心砖墓的结构图。王振锋的《汉代圹砖集录·附说》中的两张空心砖墓图，即引自关野贞的书中。

38　西汉早中晚分期，早期为汉兴至汉武帝即位前后，中期为汉武帝至汉宣帝即位前后，晚期为汉宣帝至新莽末。

39　笔者另有专文研究，待刊。

汉晚期就不见了，阳纹画像空心砖墓出现于西汉晚期，一直到新莽时期。

据此，阴纹画像空心砖墓的墓形必然是西汉中期墓的墓形，即主室为长方形，墓顶或为平顶，或是斜坡顶。那么，它究竟是平顶形墓，还是斜坡顶形墓呢？早期学者的查访、记录，或许为我们提供了有益的线索。

丁士选曾经到过挖墓现场，看到过几座空心砖墓[40]，据他所言平顶墓中只有几何纹砖和素面砖，屋形墓中才用画像砖。这一认识恰好与洛阳的考古资料相吻合。说明阴纹画像空心砖墓的形制是长方形斜坡屋脊形顶墓，如同宜阳牌窑画像空心砖墓的形制。

（二）阴纹画像空心砖墓的年代

《中国古墓砖图考》书中的阴纹画像空心砖，怀履光将其年代定为公元前3世纪，显然有误。我们断定"怀氏砖"和宜阳砖极有可能是同一制砖作坊的产品，再考虑到阳线木模的使用时间有限，这两批砖的生产时间相差不会很远，所以，它们应是同一时期的作品，即同属西汉中期，约公元前2世纪末前后。

根据砖上画像的内容，我们来考订一下画像砖的大致年代。

由考古材料可知，用空心砖造墓，洛阳地区在西汉至新莽时期一直流行。空心砖作为筑墓材料，当时有专门的作坊进行制作和出售。

洛阳发现的空心砖墓绝大多数是用素面砖和几何纹砖砌成的普通空心砖墓，画像空心砖墓数量很少。目前所见的阴纹画像空心砖的数量，总数不超过1000块。如果以1000块计算，每墓使用的画像砖按15块（如宜阳画像砖墓）至19块（左右壁8块、后壁2块、山墙砖4块、门楣1、门框2、门扉2）计算，画像砖墓的数量也就是有66至52座。这说明画像砖制作复杂、价格不菲，绝非寻常人家所用。因为价格高，使用的人群数量少，画像砖不会像普通空心砖那样大批地生产。只有有人预订，作坊才生产制作。同时，作坊工匠会根据当时的丧葬习俗和社会上的流行图案，制作出各种画像的样品供人选择。因此，画像砖上印制的画像种类因为制砖的时间、批次，甚至丧家的要求不同而存在一定的差异是完全有可能的。

---

40 "予乘假期归国之便，经介导赴发掘场所数处，访查若辈发掘之程序，并注意其椁墓之营造，当地目击，自较真实。惟无试做科学发掘之机会，且以环境限制，即照相实测，亦不可得，殊深惭汗"。丁士选：《圹砖琐言》，北平燕京大学《考古学社社刊》第六期，1937年。

在"怀氏砖"中，出现最多的画像是马。55 块砖中，有 42 块砖上有马。马是除人物之外，造型变化最多的画像，也是艺术水平最高的画像。据统计，马的造型有十三种，就是说工匠要做出十三种马的印模。那么，当时的工匠为什么对马情有独钟，要花费如此大的精力来表现马呢？我们认为这一定与西汉中期某一阶段的风尚有极大的关系。

众所周知，汉武帝特别喜爱良马，为得到西域的良马，不惜两次发动大规模的战争。汉武帝得到宝马后，分别以"西极马"和"天马"为之命名[41]，并于元狩二年（前 121）和元鼎四年（前 113），分别作《太一天马歌》和《西极天马之歌》[42]。还按照最优良的马的尺寸铸造一匹比例准确的铜马，立于长安未央宫宦者署的鲁班门外，以此铜马作为评选良马的标准，鲁班门因此改名"金马门。"上行下效，民间百姓也特别珍视、喜爱骏马，艺术家们投入满腔的热情，创作出空前绝后的艺术佳作。画像砖上马的造型分为两类，写实类和艺术夸张类。那些画出翅膀的马，表现的或许就是来自西北的所谓天马吧。这些马的画像从一个方面说明，这些画像空心砖的年代应距汉武帝获得西域优良马种的时间不远，约在元狩年间至元鼎年间（前121—前 113）。

总之，画像空心砖墓出现于西汉中期的汉武帝元狩年之后，生产的数量不多，流行时间也很短，或许只有短短几年。

以上两点认识，虽说是建立在考古材料的基础上，但这些材料中画像空心砖墓太少，尤其是只有一座阴纹画像空心砖墓。这些认识是否正确，还需要更多的考古材料来证实。

（三）画像空心砖的制作工艺

画像空心砖的制作工艺一直受到学者们的普遍关注，或询访窑工，或查阅典籍，或对墓砖详加观察，提出了不同的意见。因为画像空心砖的制作工艺早已失传，各种说法俱是推测。归纳各种意见有主要四种：

1. 拼合法。王振铎认为，先根据砖的形状做出木范，然后把陶泥放入范中，合拢作中空状，待其半干，用刀开挖两端的孔洞，然后用印模压出

---

41 "得乌孙马好，名曰'天马'。及得宛汗血马，益壮，更名乌孙马曰'西极马'，宛马曰'天马'云。"（汉）班固：《汉书·张骞传》，中华书局，1962 年。
42 王淑梅、于盛庭：《再论汉武帝天马歌的写作缘由和年代问题》，《乐府学》第五辑。

砖上的花纹[43]。

2. 掏挖法。丁士选认为，先据砖的形状做出木范，填入陶泥，做出砖坯，然后工匠用手指或狭长形的工具将砖掏挖成空心状，画像是在空心砖坯做好后用印模印上去的。他否定了民间所说的沙袋法和两块凹面砖拼合法[44]。

3. 四片黏合法。《洛阳烧沟汉墓》认为，空心砖是用"四片黏合"法制成。砖面上的花纹，皆于四片未合之前印上。烧制与一般烧砖无异，唯因砖体中空，为免烧时内中气体膨胀，故两端挖凿小孔[45]。

4. 沙袋法。黄明兰认为，画像空心砖的制作方法是沙袋法，砖坯做好后加印画像[46]。

我们根据砖上的画像，认为《洛阳烧沟汉墓》中的说法更符合实际情况，理由是：绝大多数画像砖是两面有花纹，有的砖是四面有花纹，两个主面印画像，侧面印几何纹。如果是砖坯制好后再翻动砖坯，逐面加印画像，即便是晾一段时间翻动，也有可能会对先印上花纹造成损害。我们仔细观察砖上各面的画像和纹饰，没有看到任何因挤压、翻动而造成的损坏痕迹（阳纹画像砖尤其易被损坏）。这说明，画像是在四片泥片未组合成砖之前就印上了，待其达到一定的硬度，花纹不会被损伤时再进行组合。在组合过程中弥合泥片间的接缝，最后再上两端的泥片。

关于砖上各种画像的制作方法和模具的制作、使用，怀履光先生在做过细致的观察和实验后提出了独到而精当的看法，详见本书的第六章，在此不再赘述。

摘自［加拿大］怀履光著，徐婵菲译，［加拿大］沈辰校，《中国（洛阳）古墓砖图考》，中州古籍出版社 2014 年版。

43　王振铎：《汉代圹砖集录附说》，北平考古学社刊印，1935 年。笔者按：王所言之法似乎是丁士选所谓的两块凹面砖拼合而成的拼合法。
44　丁士选：《圹砖琐言》，北平燕京大学《考古学社社刊》第六期，1937 年。
45　洛阳区考古发掘队：《洛阳烧沟汉墓》，科学出版社，1959 年。书中第二编第六章对空心砖的砖型、制作、纹饰三方面进行研究，第 84—91 页。
46　黄明兰：《洛阳汉画像砖》，河南美术出版社，1986 年。第 5—6 页。

图书在版编目（CIP）数据

砖画印像：加拿大皇家安大略博物馆藏洛阳出土西汉画像空心砖：汉、英 /
[加拿大] 沈辰，徐婵菲编 . 一北京：国家图书馆出版社，2024.4

ISBN 978-7-5013-7413-7

Ⅰ. ①砖… Ⅱ. ①沈… ②徐… Ⅲ. ①画像砖－美术考古－洛阳－西汉时代－
汉、英 Ⅳ. ①K879.44

中国版本图书馆CIP数据核字（2022）第012250号

书　　名　砖画印像：加拿大皇家安大略博物馆藏洛阳出土西汉画像空心砖
著　　者　[加拿大] 沈　辰　徐婵菲　编
责任编辑　许海燕　王燕来　王佳妍
装帧设计　■瓢文化·邱特聪

出版发行　国家图书馆出版社（北京市西城区文津街7号　100034）
　　　　　（原书目文献出版社　北京图书馆出版社）
　　　　　010-66114536　63802249　nlcpress@nlc.cn（邮购）
网　　址　http://www.nlcpress.com →投稿中心
印　　装　北京启航东方印刷有限公司
版次印次　2024 年 4 月第 1 版　2024 年 4 月第 1 次印刷

开　　本　889×1194　1 / 16
印　　张　24.5
书　　号　ISBN 978-7-5013-7413-7
定　　价　380.00 元